REMEMBER CREATION

God's World of Wonder and Delight

REMEMBER CREATION

God's World of Wonder and Delight

SCOTT HOEZEE

William B. Eerdmans Publishing Company

Grand Rapids, Michigan/Cambridge, U.K.

© 1998 Wm B. Eerdmans Publishing Co.
255 Jefferson Ave. S.E., Grand Rapids, Michigan 49503 /
P.O. Box 163, Cambridge CB3 9PU U.K.
All rights reserved

Printed in the United States of America

02 01 00 99 98   7 6 5 4 3 2 1

Library of Congress Cataloging-in-Publication Data
Hoezee, Scott, 1964–
    Remember creation : God's world of delight and wonder /
Scott Hoezee.
        p. cm.
    Includes index.
    ISBN 0–8028–4470–7 (pbk. : alk. paper)
    1. Human ecology — Religious aspects — Christianity.
    2. Creation — Biblical teaching. I. Title.
BT695.5.H64   1998
261.8'362—dc21   97–35120
                                                          CIP

Cover Art:
DIN64614 She did not turn (study),
1974 by David Inshaw (living artist)
Private Collection/Bridgeman Art Library, London

For Julianna and Graham:

May you always know worlds of wonder

CONTENTS

ACKNOWLEDGMENTS

When he asked me to comment on one of his manuscripts, acclaimed author Philip Yancey said he was seeking input because even after having published a dozen books, he knows he is still not able to write a book alone. So also this volume represents the help of many people, only a few of whom can be singled out here.

I thank my wife, Rosemary, for her own love for the creation and for all the ways by which she has infused that love into me. I thank her for pushing me to sharpen my thinking, for challenging me to act in ways that are consistent with what I have written, and for critiquing the manuscript. Rosemary also deserves credit for putting up with me when my focus on this work distracted me from more important matters.

I thank my congregation, Calvin Christian Reformed Church in Grand Rapids, Michigan. Their ongoing encouragement of my writing and their granting me six weeks of study leave during the summer of 1997 are what allowed me to write this book.

Thanks to Sandra DeGroot and William B. Eerdmans Jr. for agreeing to publish this even at a time when it existed mostly only in my mind. Their enthusiasm was invigorating throughout the writing process.

Several people took the time to read and comment on various drafts of this work. My hearty thanks to Neal Plantinga for being a cherished friend and for once again giving me such fine feedback. I thank also Philip Yancey, Rolf Bouma, and Lionel Basney. Each of them brought his own expertise to bear on the manuscript: Philip's long experience in the art of writing, Rolf's ardor for the creation combined with his formal education in environmental ethics, and Lionel's deep love for both the creation and for the English language. All helped me sharpen my thinking and my prose.

Last, I thank my children, to whom I have dedicated this book. Their own wide-eyed wonder over the creation has reminded me to become like a child again, slowing down long enough to pause over everything from anthills to acorns. In the midst of this project, my daughter's astonishment over seeing her first comet in the spring of 1997 also spoke volumes about the joy and splendor with which God has filled the cosmos. In the pages ahead I will eventually highlight the creation prophecies of Isaiah. In Isaiah 11:6 the prophet declares that in the new creation wolves, lambs, calves, and lions will coexist in perfect *shalom,* and when they do, "a little child will lead them." I am grateful for my own little children, who even now lead me into still greater love for the creation of our God.

Scott Hoezee

I will remember the deeds of the LORD; yes, I will remember your miracles of long ago. I will meditate on all your works and consider all your mighty deeds.

Psalm 77:11–12

But [the scoffers] deliberately forget that long ago by God's word the heavens existed and the earth was formed out of water and by water.

2 Peter 3:5

INTRODUCTION

That Was Then ...

Library shelves everywhere are sagging under the weight of books that deal with some aspect of creation versus evolution. Few subjects have generated as much interest (and heat) in the last thirty years as has the debate about cosmic origins. If book publications, sales, and awards are any indication, this interest is far from waning.

Indeed, *Christianity Today*'s Book of the Year for 1997 was *Darwin's Black Box* by Michael Behe — a highly technical, scientific book dealing with certain intracellular biochemical subcomponents, the complexity of which, Behe believes, could not have formed through Darwinian evolutionary development. In addition to Behe's volume, the *Christianity Today* Top 25 list for 1997 contained yet another book dealing with the subject of creation versus evolution — *The Battle of Beginnings: Why Neither Side Is Winning the Creation-Evolution Debate* by philosopher Del Ratzsch. [1]

But actually the 1997 list is not at all unusual in that these kinds of books have been appearing regularly since *Christianity Today* began compiling its annual Top 25 list. The readers who select these books each year routinely vote for volumes that critique fossil records, Darwinian theories, and the state of scientific education in public schools and universities. However, books dealing with a Christian view of ecology or celebrating the beauty of God's handiwork have never made the list.

Perhaps this is not surprising given how many more books there are available on evolution compared with stewardship and Christian ecology. A quick survey of catalogs from a few of the major Christian publishing houses reveals relatively few titles dealing with the wonders of creation or the need to preserve God's world but many titles dealing with scientific debates on varying aspects of evolutionary theory. One publisher lists eight titles in creation studies, seven of which have to do with fossils, Darwin, or Galileo and only one of which deals with Christian ecology for the world today. (It should be noted that in recent years there has been an increase in the number of books published on the subject of Christian ecology, but many of these books tend toward the academic end of the reading spectrum and so have not filtered down to the popular evangelical readership.)

The same phenomenon sometimes can be seen in public lecture venues. Some time ago I attended an outstanding lecture about the stewardship of God's precious creation. The speech was delivered by a Christian teacher and writer with a national reputation for excellence in the field of earth studies. Indeed, his prominence in ecological matters has qualified him to testify before Congress and has even brought him into regular consultations with the United States secretary of the interior. Not surprisingly, his speech bristled with fresh ideas as he harvested insights from his years of experience and hard study. Additionally, the setting for his speech was an exceedingly popular, nationally renowned lecture series known for its standing-room-only crowds. On this occasion, however, for this important speech by this prominent expert, there were empty seats — quite a few of them.

After the lecture a friend of mine lamented this less-than-stellar turnout, believing it was a sign of a larger evangelical apathy on the subject of the environment. He was probably correct. As I drove home, I recalled that a couple of years earlier this same lecture series had featured a speech on the theory of evolution versus the biblical view of creation. Not surprisingly, that lecture had garnered a huge crowd of people, many of whom had to watch the speech on monitors in overflow rooms.

Why is it that many Christians find a theological-scientific debate about creation's ancient origins far more engaging than a speech about how to live responsibly in the creation today? Why do we tend to be more tantalized by academic debates that focus our gaze on what happened long ago than we are by hands-on discussions that focus our gaze on the world of wonders outside our windows right now? How can it be that we have more interest in something as difficult as the irreducible complexity of intracellular molecular subprocesses than we have in something as comparatively simple as enjoying and preserving the humpback whale?

Granted that establishing God as the supreme creator of everything is vital. Granted that some in the scientific community use evolution as a way to undercut biblical claims to God's supremacy or to humanity's having been made in the image of God. Granted, therefore, that we Christians properly feel we have a stake in at least some aspects of the creation versus evolution debate. And granted, therefore, that many of the books published on this subject are important works written by brilliant scholars and scientists who are making a fine contribution to our larger understandings of the universe. Granted all of that, is it right that we take more interest in this ancient aspect of the creation than we do in our daily celebration and maintenance of that same creation?

A number of the books published on evolution in recent years include the word *battle* somewhere in their titles. But the particular "battle" about cosmic origins is not the only battle being waged over the creation right now — it may not even be the most significant one. As I aim to show in this book, the more significant creation battle going on right now is between God and the devil, and the battleground for this war is the present-day world of created wonders. For the Bible reveals with utter clarity and consistency not only that God made all that exists but also that he continues to adore this work, that he is even now redeeming it from the clutches of the Evil One, and that he will one day soon make a new creation of wonder and delight. This new creation will then be the eternal setting of joy in which we will live with our Creator and Redeemer God forever. All of these strands of biblical teaching are nicely braided together by Paul in the opening words to the Colossians: "For [Jesus] has rescued us from the dominion of darkness and brought us into the kingdom of the Son he loves ... for by him all things were created.... [And] God was pleased to have all his fullness dwell in him and through him *to reconcile to himself all things, whether things on earth or things in heaven....* This is the gospel ... that has been proclaimed to every creature under heaven" (Col. 1:13, 16a, 19–20, 23b, emphasis added).

So given that God loves this cosmos enough to die for it, is it any surprise to discover that the devil hates it? Given that the Son of God died to redeem the entire universe from its bondage to decay, is it any surprise that the devil even now seeks to undermine and sully the created splendors of this world? Given that one day soon God will renew everything from primroses to quasars, is it any surprise that the devil is furiously seeking to block that re-creation?

What God loves, the devil hates. But in all of the recent fascination with the process of how this world came to be, some seem to have forgotten the world that now exists. I have no doubt the devil is indeed interested in removing God from the picture of how the universe came into being long ago, but that does not preclude his also having a vicious interest in turning God's divine cosmos into a demonic chaos today. When it comes to threatening God's wonderful work of creation, promoting wrong ideas about universal origins is surely just one item on the devil's very long list of things to do each day.

Consider an analogy: Imagine a mother and father who become so enamored with thoughts about the day of their daughter's birth that they scarcely give any thought to raising the little girl once they take her home from the hospital. They spend so much time at the dinner table each evening talking about and retelling the stories surrounding her birth that they never bother to make sure she is eating nutritional meals. They are so fascinated by watching again and again the videotape taken in the delivery room that many times they fail to notice that their youngster has wandered out into the street or that she is playing with the poisons stored under the kitchen sink.

This is an admittedly absurd analogy, and yet it bears some resemblance to the ways by which recent discussions on cosmic origins have displaced our having a similarly fierce interest to care for, protect, and nourish the world that now exists all around us. For at most, right thinking about cosmic origins is just one part of our larger understanding of the universe and of our place in it. Yet many Christians today seem to forget this, working themselves into a lather about Darwin at the expense of fighting the devil's many other attempts to harm God's creation through threats like pollution and species extinction. Some seem to have so intently fixed their gaze on the moment of creation that they do not have any time left to gaze at the glorious bluebird, who even now sings God's praises in the backyard.

This book aims to show that delighting in and preserving God's creation should properly be seen as a part of daily discipleship. Further, I intend to make this point with biblical arguments. For there is actually far more material in Scripture about God's delight in his creation — and thus our need to delight in and preserve God's world — than there is about issues relating to the scientific origins of the cosmos.

Yet it is astonishing how easily we miss this facet of the Bible, sometimes quietly thinking that the Bible is mostly the story about how human souls get saved. At times it appears that some Christians conceive of salvation as an escape route out of the creation and into a heavenly realm — a realm often depicted as being as unlike this earth as is imaginable. But we need to recognize that the Bible is eminently interested in this creation — so much so that what we call "heaven" is often called simply "the new earth" in the Bible.

So in this book we will first establish what we will call the "divine delight" in the creation, and we will then use that as a goad to immerse ourselves in the knowledge and joys of this creation in imitation of our Creator God. Second, we will move beyond this delightful picture to the darker truth that the devil despises God's handiwork and so seeks to turn the creation into a nightmare of hellish havoc. We will then use this as a goad to fight the devil through our thoughtful and attentive preservation of God's world — a task which we were created in God's image to do in the first place.

More than anything, however, I hope to show clearly the biblical roots of all that follows. The better we know how the Bible presents God's creation, the more inspired we will be to get out into that world both to enjoy and preserve it. Eugene Peterson once noted that John Calvin wrote eloquently about the creation, often claiming that this world is like a grand theater of divine works. Yet, Peterson claims, despite the fact that Calvin lived and worked in Geneva, Switzerland — one of the most beautiful places in the world — there is almost no evidence from Calvin's letters or books that he ever got out of his library to plunge into the glorious mountains and valleys that ring Geneva, to revel in and soak up their wonders. [2]

My hope and prayer is that before this book draws to a conclusion, you, the reader, will have grown impatient with reading it. Of course, I hope this impatience results not from poor thinking or tedious writing on my part. Instead, I hope that the biblical thoughts expressed here will so spark your enthusiasm for the creation that you will be eager to toss this volume aside and rush out into some part of God's world, adding your voice to "all creatures here below" in praise of the Creator, from whom all blessings flow.

DELIGHTFUL THEOLOGY

God's Creation of Delight and Play

The Spider and the Bible

Some time ago, on the very week I was to begin a series of sermons on the wonders of God's creation, a startling thing happened. In that series it was my intention to tell the congregation that the Bible is our first, best source for motivation to enjoy and preserve our God's beloved cosmos. To bolster and illustrate this claim I picked up my pulpit Bible to begin that day's Scripture reading.

But no sooner did I touch the Bible than a dime-sized, yellow spider raced out from under it, skittered past my hand, and disappeared under the lip of the pulpit. Of course, I did not mention this to the congregation but simply proceeded with the Scripture reading as though nothing had happened. I must confess, however, that my first inclination was to sweep this spider away or, better yet, quietly to squash him with the Bible! After all, the pulpit is no place for an arachnid — creatures such as this belong not in church but outside. But this little fellow got away safely, never to be seen by me again.

At the risk of making too much of so commonplace an incident, that spider's surprise ecclesiastical appearance — and my initial disdain of it — reminded me that in many ways this highlights our problem as Christian worshipers of God. Too often when we gather in our churches for worship, we find ourselves far removed from the welter of creatures with whom we share this planet — so much so that even to see a spider or any creature like it in church is rare if not annoying.

Within most church's sanctuaries worshipers are cut off from the creation, proceeding through the weekly liturgy without seeing or thinking much about nature and its wonders. We gather in buildings crafted of man-made bricks, illuminated by artificial lights, and walled in by stained-glass windows — windows which, though lovely and rich in holy symbolism, point to heavenly things, not earthly ones. Also, the mere fact that these windows are made of stained glass —

6

as opposed to the clear glass of most windows — prevents us from seeing the outside world. Although the presence or absence of sunlight is noticeable through the stained-glass windows of my home congregation, not much else is. There are many occasions when, upon exiting the building after worship, we are surprised to see that it had rained or snowed at some point during the service and we had been wholly unaware of it.

Curiously, however, it was not always so for God's people when they gathered for worship. If you look closely at the descriptions of Solomon's temple in 1 Kings 6–7, you notice that the design of the temple was intended to remind the congregation of the created order. (Some commentators think the temple design was a depiction of the Garden of Eden.) Solomon's temple was filled with carvings of gourds, pomegranates, lilies, palm trees, flowers, lions, bears, and bulls. A major piece of the temple was a huge bronze sculpture depicting the ocean, including waves and sea creatures frolicking amid the carved metallic swells.

The creation was the setting for Israelite worship in ways it seldom is in modern houses of worship. So even as the Israelites praised their resplendent heavenly God, they were reminded of his earthly (and earthy) created splendors — beauties which are themselves shimmering reflections of God's own glory. God's gift of creation, replete with its wonderful fertility and abundance of exotic life, was not to be forgotten by worshipers within the confines of Solomon's temple. Rather, the creation and the congregation's offering up of praise for it were key components in Israel's liturgy.

But today this is seldom the case. A couple of exceptions that come to mind are the Willow Creek church in Illinois and the Crystal Cathedral in Garden Grove, California, two congregations which, curiously, set out to be different from typical churches. The designers of Willow Creek landscaped the grounds to include a variety of creation's beauties — including a lake — while also allowing worshipers to see those beauties through many clear-glass windows.

The Crystal Cathedral, of course, is essentially one giant window. The warm California sunlight streams freely through the all-glass edifice, allowing real plants and trees to grow indoors. Fountains in the sanctuary allow worshipers to hear sounds akin to the bubbling of brooks, and a few of the windows near the pulpit can be opened to let in fresh air and birdsong. The Crystal Cathedral is one sanctuary that at least in this respect appears to be something of an heir to Solomon's temple — a place where the congregation's acts of worship are enhanced and accented by the warmth, light, and fruitful beauty of the surrounding landscape. (Alas, however, the very feature of this church that makes it alive to the creation also creates an ecological drawback. Although built like a greenhouse, the Crystal Cathedral is meant for people, not rhododendrons. Dreadful amounts of energy are consumed to provide air-conditioned comfort in California's sizzling sunshine.)

However, the idea of providing displays of the larger creation is proper and biblical. Such reminders could be used in all Christian churches because a major part of our Christian vocation should be the nurturing of delight in this universe of wonders — a delight similar to God's own playful joy in creation, which we see traced for us in Scripture. This world teems with opportunities for such delight — the question is whether we take the time to notice. On that Sunday morning just as I was getting ready to proclaim the wonders of the creation's life on this earth, a fellow citizen of this planet made himself (or herself) known and so reminded me that we are surrounded by a colossal exuberance of life.

Indeed, some years ago scientists discovered that if you scoop up just one teaspoon of dirt from the top inch of soil, you typically can find in that little sample just over thirteen hundred living creatures, including mites, springtails, millipedes, beetles, and about a dozen other kinds of critters. If you factor in the microscopic fungi, protozoa, algae, and bacteria, the population in that little bit of dirt tops out around two billion creatures.[1] In the wider world, biologists tell us that no one is sure just what the total number of different species on this planet may be. Although some estimate there may be as many as ten- to thirty-million different species on earth, a few scientists say the number actually may be as lofty as one hundred million!

The Creation Window

We should never forget — least of all during our worship of the Creator God — that we live in a universe teeming with life-forms — creatures made by God and, therefore, also dearly loved by this same God. But for better or worse, it is unlikely that most church buildings will be renovated to have a Crystal Cathedral-like openness to the natural world. Few people would care to start punching out expensive and beautiful stained-glass windows in favor of walls of clear glass. But even without such radical retrofitting of sanctuaries, all churches already contain something that is itself a most wonderful, clear window on the creation: the Bible.

In most church services the reading and preaching of the sacred text form the centerpiece to the worship experience. And these days many people believe that the litmus test for a true Bible-believing Christian is whether a person endorses the tenet of biblical inerrancy, which claims that the Bible is without mistakes in all that it says, teaches, and reveals. But if we take this sacred book seriously, we cannot miss seeing its ardent, consistent celebration of and concern for the creation of our God. Ironically, according to a 1994 study conducted by James L. Guth and Lyman A. Kellstedt, Christian congregations that show the greatest seriousness for the Bible and are the most committed to biblical inerrancy are the very same congregations that tend to be the least concerned about ecology and are the least interested in the environment or in those programs and groups that promote its preservation. [2] The more authority a congregation ascribes to the Bible, the less affinity that congregation tends to have for environmentalists. Oddly, more liberal congregations — which tend to have lower views of Scripture, often questioning whether the Bible really is the authoritative revelation of God's will — have a much greater concern to preserve the creation. More oddly still, secular people with no ties to the Bible have been and remain the ones who are at the forefront of ecological concern.

In his book *The Greening of Protestant Thought,* Robert Booth Fowler notes that while there has been a steady increase in the number of scholarly Christian books about the environment, there has not been a similar increase in the number of popular books published on the subject. Fowler also demonstrates that although there has been a steady heightening of ecological consciousness among Christians over the past thirty years, this movement largely has been confined to the more liberal mainline denominations. Although more conservative evangelical Christians have been "catching up" in recent years — as evidenced by an increase in ecologically sensitive articles in the magazine *Christianity Today* — Fowler nevertheless uncovers the same trend identified by the Guth-Kellstedt study. [3]

Fundamentalist Christians probably represent the most conservative, Bible-based wing of American Protestantism, and not surprisingly, it is here Fowler detects attitudes ranging from indifference to outright hostility toward the environmentalist movement. Dispensationalist Christians in particular tend to spend so much time focusing on end-time scenarios of tribulations, raptures, and apocalypses that they appear to have little time or interest left to ponder the state of the creation today. For many fundamentalists, efforts to preserve the earth are just one more example of a larger "secular humanism" that Christians are all but obligated to shun. [4]

The result is that most of the major organizations now working for global ecological preservation have little or no connection to organized Christianity. It is no surprise that a number of these groups occasionally exhibit quirky, and sometimes deeply troubling, religious ideas like the need to worship "Mother Earth" or a desire to locate "god-ness" deep within ancient crystals.

When some Christians see such idolatrous, pantheistic traits within the ecological movement, they use them as reason to distance themselves from such dangerous "New Age" spiritual muddles. It is a vicious cycle: First, Christians largely ignore the physical world in favor of more "spiritual" emphases. Then when non-Christians step into the ecological vacuum with predictably non-Christian teachings, Christians hold up those teachings as evidence that they must further distance themselves from the environmentalist movement!

For much of the twentieth century, Christians have trumpeted loudly that the Bible has a great deal to say on matters relating to the creation. But this message generally has been proclaimed from the debate lectern during attempts to defeat evolutionist scientists. Although the Bible may indeed have much to contribute to a proper understanding of the universe's origins, it has far more to contribute to a proper understanding of our Christian responsibility to revel in, nurture, and sustain God's universe today. The same Bible whose revelation is so utterly authoritative for Christians is the primary window through which we can glimpse God's deep, delightful, and abiding concern for his creation — a concern that God's children must make their own.

Ending at the Beginning

My seminary professor Fred Klooster always made a point of saying, "Where you begin in theology determines where you end up." Traditionally, Christians have begun theology with the affirmation that God lovingly and grandly made everything that exists. (This is where the Bible begins, after all!) The vital importance of beginning theology properly with the doctrine of creation is what led Thomas Aquinas to write that "any error about creation also leads to an error about God." [5]

So if we begin with fundamental assertions about God as Creator and the creation as his premiere work, then we should expect to find creation figuring prominently at the end of our theological discussions as well. Properly understood as the beginning and the end of theology, the creation should also be highly visible in all of our biblical and theological reflections, in each of our Christian worship services, and at every level of our day-to-day Christian lives.

But so often it seems not very prominent at all. These days many Christians seem to begin their theology not with the creation but with the cross and resurrection of Jesus — as though the climax of salvation history trumps the significance of everything that led up to it. But if we begin with the story of redemption, we end up talking only about the redemption of people's souls, thus shortchanging the physical creation.

Even the original authors of the New Testament did not begin with the life, death, and resurrection of Jesus. Recall that when the apostle John opened his Gospel, he began by harking back to Genesis: "In the beginning was the Word [and] ... through him all things were made" (John 1:1, 3a). The Book of Hebrews also begins with creation: "[I]n these last days [God] has spoken to us by his Son ... through whom he made the universe.... In the beginning, O Lord, you laid the foundations of the earth, and the heavens are the work of your hands" (Heb. 1:2, 10).

When Paul opened his letter to the Colossians, he made this same theological-biblical move: "For by [Jesus] all things were created ... and in him all things hold together" (Col. 1:16–17). Even the last book of the Bible recalls the creation. When John reports his vision of the heavenly praise chorus to the Lamb of God, the first song he reports hearing is not the one about the redemptive blood of the Lamb but rather the song that proclaims, "You are worthy, our Lord and God, to receive glory and honor and power, *for you created all things,* and by your will they were created and have their being" (Rev. 4:11, emphasis added).

These biblical writers opened their books and letters this way because they knew that the two great themes of divine history (and hence now of Scripture) are creation and redemption. They knew what I learned in seminary: All of theology boils down to a discussion of God, creation, and their relation. Everything a Christian may wish to say or proclaim from the Bible — including the entire past, present, and future of salvation history — stems from and is encompassed by this discussion.

Yet today creation is eclipsed by redemption in a variety of ways. Sometimes this can be detected in songs and hymns. A few years ago the popular singer Sandi Patty recorded a hit song apparently based on Psalm 8. Quoting directly from the first verse of the psalm, Patty's song begins with the refrain, "O Lord, our Lord, how majestic is your name in all the earth."

Of course, the bulk of Psalm 8 fleshes out this majesty of God by pointing to the moon and the stars and all the wondrous works of God's creative hand. "When I consider your heavens, the work of your fingers, the moon and the stars, which you have set in place, what is man that you are mindful of him?"

But Patty's popular song dispenses with Psalm 8's creation celebration in favor of instead moving immediately into the New Testament and a focus on redemption in Jesus: "O Lord, our Lord, how majestic is your name in all the earth. Prince of Peace, Mighty God, O Lord God Almighty!" Unhappily, in this song a biblical focus on the creation drops from view in favor of thinking only about the salvation of human beings.

A similar phenomenon can be seen in the widely sung hymn "Beautiful Savior." In the first stanza Jesus is appropriately lauded as the "King of creation." The second and third stanzas also start out celebrating the creation by pointing to the beauty of meadows, woodlands, sun, moon, and stars. But the conclusion of both stanzas not so subtly lowers the importance of the creation compared with redemption by declaring that despite the beauty of this earth and the brilliance of the heavens, *Jesus* shines brighter, fairer, and purer than anything. Although not as blatant, this hymn is reminiscent of the song that urges, "Turn your eyes upon Jesus ... and the things of earth will grow strangely dim." The implication is that redemption through Christ makes this world — if not the whole creation generally — vastly uninteresting if not unimportant.

Sometimes, however, the eclipse of creation by redemption can be seen not only subtly in popular musical lyrics but in direct statements made by writers and theologians throughout much of the twentieth century. Among the theological giants of biblical scholarship in this century have been Gerhard von Rad, G. Ernest Wright, and Claus Westermann. But in some of their major works they claimed that even in the Old Testament it is clear that the people of Israel were far more interested in redemption than in creation. Von Rad claimed that "the faith of Israel is primarily concerned with redemption. [B]ecause of the exclusive commitment of Israel's faith to historical salvation, the doctrine of creation was never able to attain to independent status in its own right." [6] Similarly, Wright once asserted that the doctrine of creation was of limited importance to ancient Israel, paling in significance next to events like the exodus from Egypt. Westermann went so far as to say creation was not even a part of ancient Israel's statements of faith and, in Israel's mind, the creation bore no revelation of God. [7]

Happily, biblical studies has turned around in recent years. Contemporary Old Testament scholar Brevard Childs has clearly shown how vital the doctrine of creation is in the Old Testament. Indeed, as Leo Perdue sums it up in his book *Wisdom and Creation,* it is now clear to many scholars that "creation is a pervasive theme through every area of the Hebrew canon. The view that redemptive history ... takes theological priority over creation cannot be defended by reference to the Hebrew Bible itself." [8]

Not everyone agrees, however. A recent book that I will criticize occasionally is *The Cross and the Rainforest: A Critique of Radical Green Spirituality* by British authors Robert Whelan, Joseph Kirwan, and Paul Haffner. In the foreword to this volume, Father Robert Sirico of the Acton Institute — a conservative think tank in Grand Rapids, Michigan — disparages the Christian church's new focus on creation by claiming that the larger environmentalist movement should not in any way be embraced, because it consistently propagates false views of the world and of humanity's place within it. In the face of the modern focus on the environment, Sirico claims that "we do well to remember that the goal of life is salvation through faith and the avoidance of sin. To avoid sin, we must obey God's law. His first commandment to us is to have no false gods before Him." [9]

But this statement is itself a distortion. When Jesus was asked what the greatest commandment is, he said the first and greatest commandment is "to love the Lord your God with all your heart, mind, soul, and strength" (see Matt. 22:37). It is for that reason that the Westminster Confession famously proclaims the chief goal of human life is "to glorify God and enjoy him forever." Given our fallen and sinful condition, it is true we need to be saved in order to achieve this goal. But the main goal of life is not getting saved and avoiding sin but ultimately to love God.

Becoming Better Lovers

The creation deserves our loving attentiveness simply because it is the handiwork of our God that remains a source of high and holy delight to him. This is something we can establish from the Book of Genesis even before humanity's fall into sin necessitated a plan of redemption. Creation is older than redemption — it is God's first love. Thus, Christians should cherish creation simply because the Bible tells us God cherishes it.

As Neal Plantinga recently pointed out, there is a real sense in which the Bible tells us that our highest goal is to become better lovers of God. Part of what it means to be a good lover is to be attentive to and to be invested in whatever our lover does, produces, and enjoys. [10]

For instance, in healthy and strong marriages spouses take interest in each other's work and talents. If a woman is an artist, then at the end of each day, her husband will ask about her work in the studio: what she's working on, what the subject of her current painting is. He will attend art shows where his wife's paintings are displayed and will take joy if her work wins acclaim or awards. A loving husband may even try to learn something more about art history and art theory, perhaps taking an art appreciation course through a local college so he can be a better conversation partner for his wife when she talks about her work. He will also gladly go to places like the Chicago Art Institute and will listen closely as his wife explains the paintings they encounter there.

Such is the nature of true love: We attend to, learn about, take interest in, and nurture that which brings our lover joy and a sense of accomplishment. A marriage will not last long if spouses never ask each other about their respective jobs. If we are invested in our work — and most people are — we identify with it. That is why one of our first questions upon meeting someone new is, "What do you do?" Knowing what another person does helps us to discover who he or she is. But that's also why, in answer to this common query, the average person does not usually reply, "I perform plumbing tasks," but rather makes the more personal and all-encompassing statement, "I am a plumber." Our work identifies us even as we identify with our work. Hence, if a husband becomes disconnected from what his wife creates through her work, sooner or later he will find he is disconnected from his wife as a person.

According to the Bible, if you were to ask God who he is, one of his first statements of reply would be, "I am the Creator God." (That is why each of the two great ecumenical creeds of the Christian tradition, the Apostles' Creed and the Nicene Creed, refers to God as the Creator in its opening line.) The Bible begins with the story of the creation and it concludes with the promise of a new creation. In between, the Bible returns again and again to God's work of creation and to God's premiere role as the Creator, tracing out for us what that implies for our lives as followers of this God and as inhabitants of his marvelous cosmos.

The Bible is God's inspired book by which he tells us who he is. Clearly, in this self-revelation God places a premium on his beloved cosmos. As James Nash points out in his book *Loving Nature,* one of the most sublime statements in the Bible is "God is love" (1 John 4:8). If this is so, it follows that all God does is an act of love, starting with the act of creation. As Nash puts it, "All creatures, human and otherkind, and their habitats, are not only gifts of love but also products of love and recipients of ongoing love." [11]

So if we love God, we will also take a loving interest in his creation. We will ask questions about it, we will enroll in the spiritual equivalent of a "creation appreciation" course, we will gladly take time to stroll through what environmentalist author Bill McKibben once called the "museum of divine intent" that is this world. In all these ways we will show our divine Lover that we are only too happy to attend to that which brings him joy. [12]

The Beginning

> In the beginning God created the heavens and the earth. Now the earth was form-less and empty, darkness was over the surface of the deep, and the Spirit of God was hovering over the waters.
>
> Genesis 1:1–2

But now it is time to allow the Bible itself — which some have called God's long "love letter" to his people — more fully to show us how and why God takes such loving delight in the cosmos. Because as we will now see, Scripture is our first, best reason for becoming more interested in enjoying and preserving God's cre-ative handiwork. It is for this reason that ecological writers like Thomas Berry are so very wrong in their disparagement of the Bible's witness to the creation. Berry has gone so far as to say the church needs to shelve the Bible for twenty or so years so as to realign our thinking about creation in new and better ways.

But what we in the church must do today is not shelve the Bible but simply read it better in the light of the environmental crisis that has become so promi-nent in recent decades. If we do so, we will discover many rich reasons for delighting in and preserving this universe. To prove that point, there is no bet-ter place to begin than Genesis 1 and 2.

Even a brief look at the Bible's opening chapters will reveal that a delightful sense of playfulness and joy really was sewn into the fabric of the universe. For in Genesis it is clear that God is supreme over every aspect of his creation. That supremacy, however, does not remove God from this universe but rather places him squarely in the midst of everything he so attentively made. In God's supreme attention to detail; in his careful, providential ordering of the earth; and in the happy, exuberant way by which he personally blesses the creatures of this world, we can see clearly the divine delight. And if, as Genesis 1 also tells us, we have been made in the image of this God, it is a short leap to seeing that we also should pay close attention to the details of our world, delighting in what we see in a way that is fiercely reminiscent of God himself. [13]

The stage for all of Scripture is set quickly in the first two verses of the Bible. "In the beginning God." In the beginning *God!* God is where we begin. He and he alone was supreme in the beginning. He and he alone will remain supreme forever after. In these opening four words of the Bible we sense that what we will receive in Genesis — and in the entire Bible — are both deep, theological truths and comforting, pastoral truths. Already in this first sentence we sense this. No matter what happens, no matter how bad the world looks, God is here, God is supreme, and God will care for us.

The supremacy of God is further bolstered by the next line: "God created the heavens and the earth." In Hebrew literature this phrase is known as a merismus. A merismus takes the two opposite ends of a spectrum and uses them to stand for the whole. This type of phrase is similar to our saying that someone knows a certain subject from A to Z. So if we say of a farmer, "That guy can grow everything from asparagus to zucchini," we mean he can grow everything!

So also the very first verse of the Bible tells us God created the highest place (the heavens) and the lowest place (the earth), and so we are to understand that he created everything in between, too. (Of course, our modern knowledge of the broader universe does not typically lead us to think of outer space as "high" and the earth as "low" — although we may still think in these terms relative to the sky and the ground below. But the difference between ancient Israel's cosmology — their view of the universe's physical layout and structure — and our own does not invalidate the theological truth the author of Genesis is teaching here, that God made everything.)

"In the beginning God created everything." Against every atheistic claim to universal self-sufficiency, against anyone who would claim that at best God got the cosmic ball rolling but then left the universe to its own devices, against every claim that leaves God out of any corner of the picture, these ten words form a key statement of faith. "In the beginning God created the heavens and the earth." In the beginning God created everything.

You cannot remove God from the picture. God's attention and care extend to the big things like distant galaxies and to the small things like protozoa and subatomic quarks. God made it all and so still cares for it all — nothing escapes the divine notice. In the beginning, God. Throughout all creation, God. In every thing and in all things, God.

Then in verse 2 the writer gets more specific by employing words freighted with theological meaning. The earth was "formless and empty." The Hebrew words of this verse are *tohu wabohu,* which in the rest of the Bible will become synonymous with the wilderness or desert. Anything that is *tohu wabohu* is chaotic, dangerous, the place where evil runs wild. In the Bible the desert or wilderness is the place where faith is tried, is the place where Israel was tested, is the place of exile, is the place where even Jesus was tempted by Satan. The wilderness is the place where demons howl and where faith can tatter, and so the wilderness was greatly feared by ancient peoples. Thus it is vital that we recognize God is not threatened by this demonic chaos at the beginning of the Bible; God is supreme over it and can speak this chaos out of existence. In fact, God replaces the chaos with his cosmos.

But before we get to that good news, we first see that the picture of primordial chaos is deepened in the next phrase through the mention of darkness and deep waters. For in the ancient world both the dark and the sea were viewed as forces of evil. The roiling sea and the deep darkness of the night were thought to be remnants of primordial evil, pockets of chaos in this world.

So in this second verse we are given a stark picture of all that is frightening and threatening, of all that is inhospitable to human life and flourishing. Yet over the chaos, above the deep waters and in the midst of the terrifying darkness, broods the very Spirit of God, assuring us that we are never alone — not through the deep waters, not in the dark chaos. In all creation, over and above and beyond all creation, God is here — he was here in the beginning and he is still here now. Some things never change.

In Supremely Good Order

> And God said, "Let there be light," and there was light. God saw that the light was good, and he separated the light from the darkness.
>
> Genesis 1:3

> And God said, "Let there be an expanse between the waters to separate water from water." So God made the expanse and separated the water under the expanse from the water above it. And it was so.
>
> Genesis 1:6

In the beginning God. He alone is supreme. He is not hushed or shut up by chaos. And so, starting in verse 3, God speaks the cosmos into being. God continues to speak through six "days" of creation, and each day highlights various aspects of God's order, supremacy, and delightful blessing of the creation's wild abundance of life. Short of making a thorough commentary on each verse in Genesis 1, we can pause at certain junctures in the text to retrieve some of this passage's deepest theological and most comforting pastoral truths.

First, God's divine speech brings a profound order to the creation. Notice how often the word *separate* occurs in Genesis 1. Several times we read how God separates waters from waters, separates darkness from light, separates waters from dry ground. Why is this important? Because it tells us that in the midst of chaos, God was carving out cosmos. God is in charge, pushing back chaos, removing at will the threats to *shalom* (peace). God is in charge, taking care of us tenderly by making a world that will be safe and secure.

For that same reason it is significant to note that on the second day of creation, as recorded in verses 6–8, nothing new is created. Day two is a day of merely moving things around, of organization and reorganization, of separating water from water to make oceans and sky. Again, the pastoral significance is to assure us that God is in charge, carefully, thoughtfully, and intentionally ordering a cosmos of *shalom* for all his creatures.

Second, the author of Genesis skillfully reveals God's supremacy through the sequence in which God creates the universe's splendors. On the first day, God creates light, but he is not said to make a sun or any stars. He just makes light. Here the author is sending a clear message to anyone tempted to worship the sun, moon, or stars. For Genesis tells us that the universe's true God is so great he makes light without the aid of any proximate sources of illumination. God is the original dazzler, the first cosmic source of light and of all the life it gives.

Indeed, the sun and stars are not created until the fourth day, yet plants and vegetation begin to grow on the third day. We know green plants need the sun and the process of photosynthesis to grow — even ancient peoples, though lacking our more complete knowledge of plant chemistry, knew that without sunlight plants do not grow. But the author of Genesis wants us to recognize that God is the true source of all life and growth. The true God is so great he can make plants grow without the sun — just the loving gaze of God makes things come alive.

Whenever I ponder this idea, I am reminded of a scene from the movie *E. T.: The Extraterrestrial.* In this story we meet gentle aliens from outer space who are botanists and horticulturalists, visiting earth to collect plant specimens. These creatures are experts in making plants grow. At one point in the film the alien E. T. sees a pot of flowers withering and wilting in a darkened room. So he gazes intently at the plant, widening his eyes in intensity, and the plant stand ups straight, new color and life infusing each petal of every flower. When E. T. walks away, the flowers are once again in glorious, full bloom.

Long before God creates the sun, he gazes at the green vegetation and colorful flowers he has made. As he stares lovingly at these living creatures, he widens his eyes and intensifies his divine gaze only to have the plants bloom and flourish in the warmth of his sight. God, the author of Genesis is telling us, is life itself.

By the fourth day, when God gets around to making the sun, it is almost anticlimactic. The real wonder becomes not the sun but the fact that we already had light and growth without the sun! Verse 16 contains a wonderful line: "He also made the stars." Here is a classic example of dramatic understatement. Quintillions of nuclear furnaces pierce the darkness of outer space, spewing the heat, light, and radiation of their hydrogen-helium fission. But the author mentions it in passing, as though God hardly broke a sweat in creating these bright wonders. In the beginning God. Enough said.

Divine Play

> God said, "Let the water teem with living creatures and let birds fly above the earth across the expanse of the sky." ... [And] God blessed them.
>
> Genesis 1:20, 22a

Third, let us consider Genesis's consistent presentation of God's blessing of his wildly fruitful creation. For on days five and six things really get rolling. God creates an abundance of exuberant life, making a world teeming with creatures of all kinds. One Hebrew expert notes that verse 20 legitimately could be paraphrased, "And God made the earth swarm with swarming swarms of creatures!" The language shows God's piling up the creatures on the earth.

Today we do not often get to see such swarms of creatures, but not so long ago this was still possible. In *Undaunted Courage* historian Stephen Ambrose recounts the Lewis and Clark expedition of 1804–06. According to the diaries kept by these pioneering explorers of the American West, God's "swarms of swarming swarms" were still visible in the early years of the nineteenth century. Meriwether Lewis frequently chronicled seeing herds of buffalo so huge they stretched out of sight. One day some migrating passenger pigeons flew overhead in a flock so dense it blocked the light of the sun. (It is astonishing and tragic that the passenger pigeon would be extinct less than a century later.) One day Lewis and Clark were shocked to see the wide Missouri River clotted with a white, fluffy substance. They quickly realized these were millions of feathers. As they followed a bend in the river, they discovered the source: an enormous rookery of molting white pelicans!

Such a world exploding with life is what Genesis 1 presents. There we see God blackening the skies with flocks of birds, covering the prairies with herds of cattle, and playfully filling up the oceans with whales and reefs and fishes of all types.

It is curious that the author of Genesis singles out oceans as an example of exuberant, hyperabundant life. For without the benefit of scuba gear, the ancient people never got a good look at the underwater world. (Indeed, landlocked people like the Israelites appear to have feared the sea mightily and stayed away from it whenever they could.) But we now know the oceans truly are perfect examples of the teeming of life-forms Genesis is talking about. If you have ever snorkeled or gone scuba diving over coral reefs, you know how mind boggling is the reef's display of wonderful life.

Of course, the reefs themselves are alive. A coral reef may look like no more than dead stone and rock, but the reef is actually many colonies of living polyps which create the hard, stony coral as their outer shells. Once or twice a year these polyps spawn, and when they do, they shoot into the ocean gigantic clouds of sperm and egg, briefly transforming the sea into a verdant soup of reproducing life so thick you can hardly see through it. The swarms of swarming swarms really are well seen in the oceans.

As I was preparing to write this book, my wife and I took a snorkeling trip to the Caribbean island of Bonaire. Unlike some Caribbean islands, Bonaire is not a posh tourist destination of luxury hotels and miles of sparkling white beaches. Located only fifty miles from South America, Bonaire is actually a rather stark, desert island. Bonaire's appeal lies below the water, where it explodes with life on some of the best, lushest coral reefs in the world. As we cruised silently over these reefs, we were stunned again and again at how busy the reef is. At any given moment it was difficult to know where to look as colorful fish of all shapes and sizes darted in and out of our line of vision.

Before you can fully take in the many bright colors on the stoplight parrotfish, a bright orange cardinalfish (usually a nocturnal fish) zips out of a crevice for a rare daytime appearance. Swimming over to investigate this nice sighting, you might see a moray eel peek out from yet another hiding place only to be upstaged by the mind-boggling, iridescent brilliance of a queen angelfish. And so it goes without ceasing. In less than a week we had seen thousands upon thousands of reef fish, managing to identify well over a hundred species of them (only a small percentage of the variety of marine life on coral reefs worldwide).

This is the exuberant world God made, and this is the world God blessed. As much as anything else in Genesis 1, what is most striking is the "theology of blessing" that emerges. Several times we are told God "blesses" the creatures he has made. God looks at chickadees and angelfish, at blue herons and pilot whales, at human beings and bobcats, and he blesses them. As Walter Brueggemann points out, "The creation narrative is a statement about the *blessing God has ordained into the processes of human life*. The world is a vehicle for the blessings God has ordained in it as an abiding characteristic" (emphasis in original).[14]

In this way Genesis provides us with an image we rarely think of when regarding the natural world: Hovering over the creation, brooding over this world now as surely as at the dawn of time, is the Spirit of God, hands upraised in a divine benediction. What a loaded image to keep before us when we are out and about in the world! After all, anything God blesses should be treated with utter respect and holy awe, with preserving care and joyful delight.

As I gaped at the colorful creatures that surge around the reef-lined shores of Bonaire, I found it moving to imagine my Lord smiling over the same creatures, blessing their busy swimming and eating and reproducing, delighting in their antics, being dazzled by the colors he himself dappled onto them with his divine artist's brush at the dawn of time.

"He blessed them." If, as Christians believe, receiving the divine benediction is the best thing in the world, then it is highly significant that long before God created human beings in his own image, he gave out his very first benedictory blessing to our fellow creatures on this planet.

Finally in Genesis 1 comes day six, when the land animals are created by God with equal exuberance and abundance. Ultimately, human beings are created as the crown of creation. Although God speaks all of creation into being, only the man and the woman are also spoken *to* by God. Only humanity is given the image of God so that we can enjoy this world even as God enjoys it. Of course, as we will see, a big part of what this image means is that we are charged to tend and keep the world God made, and we are to do so in ways reminiscent of God's own style of preserving creation.

God delights in this world. We find images of his joy and delight in Genesis 1. God took leisurely delight in making this cosmos. Over and over he declares his work "good," capping it off on the sixth day with the still grander declaration that the entire creation is "very good." As Brueggemann says, this goodness is not primarily to be thought of as a moral quality but rather as an aesthetic one. God delighted in how beautiful the creation turned out to be. "[The word *good*] might better be translated, 'lovely, pleasing, beautiful.'" [15]

For this reason, when God "rested" on the seventh day, it was not — as we sometimes picture it — because he was tired and needed to curl up for a post-creation Sunday afternoon nap. No, Sabbath for God was a time to kick back and watch in joyful delight all that he had made. The soaring of the eagle, the breaching of the humpback, the buzzing of the bee, the craning of the giraffe's neck — it all brought joy to God.

As theologian Daniel Migliore has written, "We often speak of creation as the work of God. It may be more helpful to think of the creation of the world as the 'play' of God, as a kind of free artistic expression whose origin must be sought ultimately in God's good pleasure." [16] There is indeed in Genesis 1 a theology of delight. God takes glee in the swarming of the swarms. It is small wonder that the more poetic creation passages in the Bible speak of how the stars "sang together for joy" on the day they were made, how the creation praises God in the clacking of tree branches and the bubbling of brooks. For God made this cosmos to be an exuberant display of wonderful life.

The Rescue of Creation

Before we complete our look at Genesis, we must note the darker element of the Bible's opening chapters: the advent of human sin. The Bible's delightful portrait of God's exuberant creation continues for just two chapters only to be interrupted by Adam and Eve's fall. Already in Genesis 3 we see introduced what must become the Bible's second major theme: redemption.

Earlier in this chapter we noted how the theme of creation frequently gets eclipsed by redemption. However, it is clear from the Bible itself that one cannot consider the theme of redemption without thinking also about creation. For the creation is what is redeemed. The God who lovingly made and who still adores this entire cosmos has no interest in redeeming us out of this universe but instead saves the creation so as to remake it into a fitting, well-ordered home — a cosmos, the nature of which we see in Genesis.

One of Scripture's earliest indications of the earthly nature of salvation comes in the Bible's second book, Exodus. As Terrence Fretheim has brilliantly noted, the Book of Exodus not only follows Genesis, it is clearly intended by the biblical authors to be a sequel to Genesis — as part 2 of the story that began when God said, "Let there be light." Seen this way Exodus becomes not simply a local, limited story of the nation of Israel's rescue from Egypt but a cosmic story through which God is redeeming the entire creation.

As Fretheim points out, creation themes from Genesis crop up again and again in the story of the exodus. One of the more prominent of such themes is rescue from the waters of chaos. As Genesis 1 makes clear, one of God's principal acts in the creation was putting the dreadful waters of chaos in their place. Hence, one of the worst fallouts of evil's presence in our world — as seen best in the flood story — is that God's creation barriers are eroded, cracked, and sometimes removed altogether. The primordial waters of chaos sometimes slip out of place and so threaten this creation's life and flourishing. God created this cosmos by pushing back the deep waters of precreation chaos. Now that evil has come, we need to be rescued out of those waters of chaos once again.

So in the Book of Exodus, when the baby Moses is rescued out of the waters of the Nile River — in which so many Israelite babies were being brutally drowned — we hear echoes of the creation story. When the Israelites are snatched out of the clutches of the Egyptian army by being led through the Red Sea on dry ground, we see a story of re-creation as God once again pushes back the waters of chaos so as to carve out a safe niche of cosmos for his people. In both of these stories we also see a foreshadowing of the New Testament practice of baptism — in Christ we are safely brought through the waters of destruction and so become "new creations" through the cleansing tide of the Lamb's shed blood. The apostle Paul makes this connection explicitly when he writes to the Corinthians, "Our forefathers were all under the cloud and ... they all passed through the sea. They were all baptized into Moses in the cloud and in the sea" (1 Cor. 10:1-2).

It is significant to note that in Exodus, when God fights Pharaoh — who clearly represents the complete anticreation forces of death and chaos — the weapons God uses are the weapons of creation. The plagues of bloody rivers, flies, gnats, darkness, frogs, and hail all make clear that this creation is the stage for salvation; the creation is the place where salvation takes place because the creation is the very object of salvation.

That is why, following the exodus, the rest of the Bible's images for salvation center on the created world. To what does God finally lead his people following their rescue from Egypt? To a good *land* filled to overflowing with abundances of every kind. As Fretheim puts it, "Redemption is in the service of creation, a creation that God purposes for all. Because God is a God of life and blessing, God will do redemptive work should those gifts be endangered. *The objective of God's work in redemption is to free people to be what they were created to be.* It is a deliverance, not from the world, but to true life in the world" (emphasis in original). [17]

Similarly, Larry Rasmussen notes that in the Old Testament, redemptive events always center on the creation. God shows up in a bush, in a spring, in an earthquake, on a mountaintop, in the wind. The primary ritual for ancient Israel was that of sacrifice in which the firstfruits of the creation are offered up to God. Religion in the Old Testament frequently seems hard to distinguish from good highlands agriculture, from proper treatment of topsoil and animals, from joyful celebration over bountiful harvests and the warm glow one gets from a goblet of fine wine.

As Rasmussen says, the reason the prophets ultimately predict our beating swords into plowshares is not only to end bloody warfare on the earth but also to enable us to return to our true calling: earthkeeping, tending the garden of God's creation! [18] Considering what we learned in this chapter about the tender, delightful ways by which God made and now preserves this creation, it is finally unsurprising to discover the rest of the Bible showing God working himself literally to death to redeem that creation. This universe is too good to let go.

"All the Worlds"

Recently scientists simultaneously shocked and titillated the world by announcing that fossils in a rock from the planet Mars indicate that there may once have been life on Mars — perhaps there still is. Though the tiny bacteria-like lifeforms found in this rock are a far cry from the little green men of Martian mythology and Hollywood movies, the mere fact that we had confirmed for the first time that some kind of life exists on another planet created a sensation. Some months later it was announced that a liquid ocean may well exist beneath the icy crust of Jupiter's moon Europa — an ocean that also may well harbor some kind of plant or animal life.

In the wake of these discoveries, a newspaper reporter asked Fuller Seminary president Richard Mouw for his reaction. This reporter was perhaps hoping to find Dr. Mouw flummoxed by these developments. After all, once upon a time Christians held that the earth is the center of the universe and is also the only home to any kind of life. If so, this reporter may have thought, perhaps some Christians would find the discovery of extraterrestrial life-forms to be deeply troubling. But far from being surprised or shaken, Mouw simply quoted from the hymn "How Great Thou Art." "O Lord, my God, when I in awesome wonder consider all the worlds thy hands have made!" [19] In other words, if there is life on Mars, we Christians will not be surprised! It would simply be so typical of God to pepper the rest of the universe with creatures even as he has done on this planet.

Given the Bible's presentation of God as the fount of a cosmos that fairly teems with swarms of swarming swarms, it is no threat to discover life all over the place — even on Mars! For God loves a lively universe. God blessed and still blesses the abundance of all life in a creation whose sheer variety and splendor bring joy to him and which should, therefore, bring delight to us as well.

Let's Play

Making God's Delight in the Creation Our Own

Paying Delightful Attention

Simone Weil once wrote that one of the deepest dimensions of the Genesis account of creation is the revelation that "God is good because he delights in the existence of something other than himself." [1] As the only creatures made in the divine image of this God, we have the ability likewise to revel in and preserve the creation of our great God. Some of the ecological implications of that ability will be traced in the coming chapters. But for now, following our pondering of the wonders of Genesis 1's theology of delight, we need to reflect on how well we ourselves take delight in the other creatures and features of this cosmos. Is this characteristic of God on display in us?

For if, as Weil suggests, a part of God's own goodness is his ability to transcend himself in order to delight in others, then a part of the divine image in us is likewise our God-given, godlike ability to transcend ourselves in order to take note of creatures not like us. So far as we know, only human beings can do this. Whitetail deer in the deep forest may live side by side with creatures like the wood thrush, but as far as we can tell the deer never spend any time contemplating this bird. The wood thrush's liquid melodies may fill the forest, but there is no evidence that deer ever stop their ordinary activities to soak up and appreciate the bird's song. (Of course, the deer do hear the song. What precisely they make of it we do not know. However, it is surely a good, natural sound that does not cause a deer to startle or shoot up its white tail in fear, as would happen were a person to speak in the forest.) Similarly, bald eagles may use their superior eyes to look for fish to scoop out of the water for dinner, but they never use those same eyes to make a study of tide pools or to ponder the behavior of humpback whales.

Only we appear able to do the godlike thing of studying, knowing, and delighting in otherness. It is for this same reason John Calvin occasionally pointed out that one of the reasons God created human beings to stand upright is precisely so we can lift our gaze to the heavens, praising God for the celestial wonders we see in the night sky. Our very posture, Calvin suggested, helps us to reach out and appreciate otherness!

As creatures made in God's likeness, this is at once our privilege and our task. There is joy out there in the creation of our God. As image bearers, it is our holy vocation to notice it, love it, revel in it, and preserve it. But do we? Or in our technological world are we often content to live cut off from the created order?

As Elizabeth Achtemeier has poignantly asked, are we more enamored with a microchip from Intel than we are with a seed from which grows a cornstalk? Do some today spend more time looking at colorful home pages on the Internet than they do absorbing the natural colors on bird wings and tulip petals? Why do millions go to Florida just to see a mechanical shark at the Universal Studios theme park but so few go to Florida to marvel over the real-life, endangered manatees in the nearby Everglades? Why do so many people travel to the West not to gasp at the majestic deserts and mountains but instead to duck into darkened Las Vegas casinos to gamble their life away? [2]

Indeed, in some places there has been in recent years an odd attempt to "bring the outdoors indoors" as a kind of cheap substitute for actually getting out and enjoying the true creation. A couple of years ago the news reported on a new pleasure palace in Japan that features an indoor ski slope with fake snow as well as an imitation ocean beach created by truckloads of sand and a huge wave machine. As one reporter noted, it is ironic that so many people were flocking to this fake beach illumined by a huge incandescent sunlamp when the real ocean was only a couple of miles away! Similarly, some of the newest casinos in Las Vegas have been decked out with fountains, arboretums of mostly plastic plants, and giant ceiling murals depicting blue skies, clouds, and sunshine.

But why do we tend to take vacations to places that are not a part of God's creation but are instead man-made imitations — cheap throwbacks to the natural world? Why go to these places when the genuine article is readily available in national, state, and even city parks? Of course, not everyone goes to such artificial environments. In the United States, national parks have seen a great increase in visitors in recent years — so much so that the landscape is in danger of being deteriorated by the plodding of too many feet. This is a problem in need of attention, but at least it indicates some heightened interest in the natural world.

Even here, however, the news is not all good; we occasionally see artificial amusements trumping the popularity of natural wonders. According to an

August 1997 article in the *New York Times*, a few years ago people who traveled to the area in and around Gatlinburg, Tennessee, did so primarily to soak up the wonders of the Great Smoky Mountains National Park. That, however, was before Dolly Parton built her "Dollywood" theme park in nearby Pigeon Forge. Now the once-sleepy Pigeon Forge, population four thousand, attracts ten million visitors annually, but many of them never make it into the national park. As the *Times* reported it, "With shopping, attractions, and 9 live music theaters, soon to be 10, many visitors here do not visit the national park at all, or zip in and out for what locals call 'a windshield experience.'" One visitor who never managed to get into the national park said, "There was so much to do that I just ran out of time." [3]

In so much of our lives — both our ordinary, everyday lives as well as our leisure hours — we too often live cut off from the creation. Instead, we immerse ourselves in the technology of the Internet, in the entertainment proffered by Blockbuster Video, in indoor environments like shopping malls and casinos, or the artificial environment of an amusement park.

Or to bring us back to where we began in the last chapter: Why do we Christians so seldom think creation thoughts even when gathered for worship? God has placed us in a world of wonders. It is our job as self-conscious image bearers to transcend ourselves in order to notice these wonders. Isn't it also our job to raise our children in such a way that they learn to see the world with God's eyes, to appreciate the wonders God made? As the authors of the book *Redeeming Creation* put it, "[I]t is hypocrisy for a Christian to willfully live separated from God's creation and the joy of it." [4]

The More You Know

As Christians we believe the image of God has been renewed in us through Jesus, who is the perfectly expressed image of God. But when in Colossians 1:15–16 the apostle Paul talks about Jesus as the image of God, he immediately connects this image to the creation. "He is the image of the invisible God, the firstborn over all creation. For by him all things were created … all things were created by him *and for him*" (emphasis added).

Apparently, part of what it means to be created in God's image is to have the ability to appreciate fully the other creatures that spring from God's creative imagination. Since in Christ this image has been reinvigorated and restored, we Christians should find our ardor for the creation likewise increasing as we gain an ever-greater degree of Christlikeness. Paul tells us that the creation was made *for* the Son of God. It belongs to him! So if the cosmos exists for Jesus' enjoyment and delight, we can safely assume our Lord himself is wonderfully alive to all of this creation's delightful details. Making ourselves similarly alive to the creation is, therefore, a holy, Christlike activity.

Parents, teachers, and preachers especially have a great opportunity and responsibility to make themselves alive to the wonders of creation in order to infuse such enthusiasm into the children, students, and parishoners under their care and tutelage. For all Christians should be naturally curious about God's creation. We should have a hunger and a longing to know more about this world and our place in it. John Calvin once wrote, "There is no doubt that the Lord would have us uninterruptedly occupied in holy meditation; that while we contemplate in all creatures, as in mirrors, his wisdom, justice, goodness, and power, we should not merely run over them cursorily and, so to speak, with a fleeting glance; but we should ponder them at length, turn them over in our minds seriously and faithfully, and recollect them repeatedly. For there are as many miracles of divine power ... as there are kinds of things in the universe."[5]

Precisely this sense of holy curiosity is something we are all born with. We all know that children are great ones for asking questions like, "Why is the sky blue?" or "Daddy, what is that?" or "Does God have skin?" But we also know that this sense of wonder can either be further developed or it can be eroded to the point of disappearing.

Many of us know adults who take no interest in things outside of their own narrow field of work and who are barely interested even in that. Some of us know people who have zero interest in the created world, who are bored with mountains, who yawn over lakes and streams, who at best give birds and wildlife that "fleeting glance" to which Calvin referred. Some of us know people who will drive 60 miles per hour through a national park's scenic drive just "to get it over with." I would suggest that something, somewhere got damaged in such people; some wire got crossed, some synaptic connection snapped and stifled their God-given sense of wonder.

Among the many holy tasks of Christians is to foster, nurture, and develop children's God-given sense of curiosity in such a way that it will still be there when they are adults. For this whole world belongs to God — we should want to know more about it.

James Nash writes that in human relationships a major part of what it means to be in love with someone is to have a desire really and fully to understand the beloved one. [6] A wife quite naturally takes an ardent interest in understanding her husband — she is curious about what makes him tick, is sensitive to avoid those things that cause him pain while also trying to promote those things that make him laugh and bring him joy. Good lovers understand each other and are forever seeking to deepen that understanding simply because true love always makes you want to know more about your beloved.

So also with creation: If we are to be lovers of God, we should want to understand creation and know more and more about it so that we can enjoy it even more. In human relationships of love, the more you know about the other person, the deeper the bond between you becomes. The more thorough your understanding of another person is, the more you "get out of" that person when you are with him or her — your conversations will be deeper and more meaningful, the activities you plan together will be more enjoyable simply because both people's likes and dislikes will be known and taken into account.

With the created world it is likewise the case that the more you know about the creation, the more you will get out of your experiences in it. Such increased understanding creates a snowball effect, a synergy of learning. Some years back, when we took our first trip to a Caribbean island, my wife and I did not give much thought to snorkeling. We knew we would probably give it a try but had no idea what it would be like or whether we would be any good at it. But once we tried it, our eyes were opened to that amazing world of vibrant life and brilliant colors. We were hooked. Still, on that first trip we mostly just took in the underwater sights.

After returning home, however, we immediately began reading up on reefs, fish, fish behavior. So on our next trip, as well as on all subsequent excursions, we have noticed an enormous boost in our enjoyment of the experience. Of course, we see many of the same things we did on our first trip, but the experience has become immensely richer and fuller. Why? Because we know so much more now. We can now identify most of the fish we see. We are now alert to watch for certain behaviors and we know what they mean; we know where to look to discover hidden things we had not seen or even known about before.

The more you know, the more you get out of something. Those who have studied art get far more out of a visit to a Monet exhibit than those who cruise through the museum only glancing at the pictures. Those who know music get far more out of a violin performance by Itzhak Perlman than people who only listen for a tune. Those who understand the nuances and rules of baseball enjoy a game far more than someone who only sees some men tossing a little white ball back and forth.

What all Christians need to develop if they are to have a godlike delight in the creation is what Sallie McFague has called "attention epistemology," meaning simply that we need to stop our busy lives long enough to peer out into the world; stop long enough to stare into tide pools and forests to see what is really there. The longer you look and the closer you pay attention, the more you will see. And the more you see, the better poised you will be to give intelligent, informed, pointed praise to the Creator for all the specific wonders he has made.

To illustrate this principle, McFague quotes these winsome lines from writer Annie Dillard. One day Dillard went to the pet shop and bought a goldfish for twenty-five cents. Here are her reflections on this simplest of all pets and this cheapest of all pet-shop purchases.

> [I named my goldfish Ellery.] He is a deep red-orange, darker than most goldfish. He steers short distances mainly with his slender red lateral fins. It took me a few days to discover his ventral fins; they are completely transparent and all but invisible — dream fins. He also has a short anal fin, and a tail that is deeply notched and perfectly transparent at the two tapered tips. He can extend his mouth so that it looks like a length of pipe; he can shift the angle of his eyes in his head so he can look before and behind himself. For this creature I paid 25 cents. I handed the man a quarter and he handed me a knotted plastic bag bouncing with water in which the goldfish swam. This fish — two bits' worth — has a coiled gut, a spine radiating fine bones, and a brain. Just before I sprinkle his food flakes into his bowl, I rap three times on the bowl's edge; now he is conditioned and swims to the surface when I rap. And, he has a heart. [7]

As Christians, particularly any of us who are in positions of education such as teaching and preaching, we must have just this kind of spiritual vision to catch sight of and revel in such common wonders with wide-eyed delight. Taking a cue from God's own wide-eyed wonder over his handiwork, remembering that this creation exists for Jesus, and recognizing that we have been made in God's image in part so that we also can delight in God's world, we should recognize that nurturing joy in the creation is our spiritual vocation — our job!

Indeed, there may even be hidden dangers to our not living in this way. Philosopher Thomas Morris notes there may well be a good reason why atheism has so often been a primarily urban phenomenon in history.

Rural people tend to be more religiously inclined. Why is that? Is it because of the greater sophistication of urban populations? I think the explanation is much more interesting. The city dweller lives in a humanly designed and constructed place. He walks on sidewalks. He gets his water from the city water works, his light from the electric company, fuel from the gas company, food from the grocer. He is insulated in a web of human interdependency. It can seem to such a person that 'man is the measure of all things,' that humanity is self-sufficient, that his only dependencies are on other people and the product of their hands. The country dweller, however, lives on the edge of human control, is in closer touch with nature, with its wonders and its terrors, with the non-human and the greater-than-human. [8]

If it is hypocritical for Christians willfully to separate themselves from the creation, we now see that it may even be spiritually dangerous. Something of our God-consciousness may be eroded by immersing ourselves only and always in man-made environments. A similar idea is communicated in one of the most famous of all poems about the creation: Gerard Manley Hopkins's "God's Grandeur." In one part of the poem, Hopkins laments our human tendency to sear, blear, and smear God's good world with our pollution. But Hopkins then includes one intriguing line: "the soil is bare now, *nor can foot feel, being shod*" (emphasis added).

Hopkins appears to be saying that in addition to the calamity of pollution is the further problem of our now being that much farther removed from God's grandeur in the creation. Even our very shoes put yet one more layer between us and the soil such that our feet cannot feel or sense the soil's barrenness. If only we understood the world more, if only we connected ourselves to it more consistently as God would have us to do, perhaps we would delight in it more and pollute it less.

In a day when "virtual reality" computer games are becoming all the rage, we Christians need to be acutely aware that there is no substitute for the true reality of getting out into and paying delightful and delighted attention to the wonders God has made. Surely God pays such close attention. Surely the Son of God for whom this creation was made pays attention in this way. Why would we want to do anything less?

Nurturing Our Delight in the Creation

Poet Maya Angelou once wrote that she is always astonished to hear someone say, "I am a Christian." In response Angelou always wants to say, "Already!?"[9] Angelou's underlying idea is that being a Christian is a vocation — a calling to certain practices, disciplines, and habits that gradually yield an increasing degree of Christlikeness. But fulfilling that calling takes a lifetime and then some. Christians never just *are,* they are also always *becoming.* Christians never assume they have the walk of Christ all sewn up but must always strive for heightened spiritual sensitivities, greater zeal for God and his works, and an ever-growing resemblance to Jesus.

So if God delights in his handiwork, how can we imitate God by taking similar delight in the creation? If being a Christian in God's cosmos means cultivating an attention epistemology that notes and revels in everything from a twenty-five-cent goldfish in a bowl to a distant comet in space, what are some concrete, hands-on ways we can do just this within the context of our busy day-to-day lives?

First, in our individual lives we could begin by planning vacations that will take us farther into the created world instead of farther away from it. We should plan to go to a national park or some other such place of created wonders at least as often — and preferably more often — as we would go to a place like Disneyworld, Hollywood, or New York City. We should spend our weekends at least as often bird-watching or hiking in local forests as strolling through the local mall.

Increasingly, we live and work in urban or suburban environments of concrete and steel — places where the vital exuberance of this planet's life is at best reduced to a faint tracing of the exotic original and is at worst obliterated from sight altogether. City landscapers and shopping mall architects may plan for flower beds or rows of trees, but these are often small, controlled areas where the true abundance of God's creation is muted and tamed. They are also areas where few if any animals or birds can be seen.

Of course, once in a while city planners will try for a little more creation variety, but it does not always work out very well. Some years ago it was discovered that the endangered peregrine falcon could be introduced into urban environments because the tops of city buildings provide a nesting site similar to the rocky scrapes and ledges where peregrines nest in the wild. Furthermore, peregrines are a natural predator of the one creature most cities have altogether too many of: pigeons. But in addition to the unhappy fact that the peregrines kept killing themselves by flying into the clear glass windows of office buildings and skyscrapers, diners in outdoor restaurants found it less than appetizing to have pigeon feathers and entrails dropping into their endive salads from the peregrine's own dining room high atop an adjacent building! In many cities, the peregrines have now been relocated to the wild.

But that is exactly where we also need to go if we truly wish to gasp in wonder at the wild abundance that springs from God's endless creation imagination. We must immerse ourselves in the genuine article — rocky seacoasts, coral reefs, sand dunes, forests, and mountains. There is no substitute for the richness of this planet's life or for the playful, godlike joy often exhibited by the birds, fish, and animals that surround us.

In her most recent book, *Super, Natural Christians,* Sallie McFague refers to what writer Robert Pyle once called "the extinction of experience." We no longer have much direct contact with the creation, and this lack of physical immersion in the world tends to make us apathetic even when we hear about ecological threats. While I was working on this book, the great undersea explorer Jacques Cousteau died. Years ago when Cousteau first began making his now-famous undersea film documentaries, a reporter asked him why he was doing it. Cousteau claimed he knew of no better way to fight the pollution of our seas and oceans than to make people aware of the wonders that are there. Cousteau was convinced that if people only knew more about the wonderful life that teems beneath the water, they would become passionately interested in preserving the oceans.

Christians, of all people, should be interested in learning about the wonders of God's world. There is no better way to accomplish this learning than by actually getting out into the creation — to revel in it and to preserve it. We should accept no substitute for hands-on experiences in God's marvelous creation.

Some years ago a member of my congregation noted my occasional sermon references to birds and bird-watching and so loaned me some binders in which he had carefully placed his back issues of a popular bird-watcher's magazine. This particular periodical was renowned for its glorious full-color photographs of North American birds. I enjoyed looking through the pictures, noting the birds I had already seen as well as those I dearly wanted to see in the wild but had not yet spotted.

When I returned the magazines, I thanked him warmly and also asked if he had ever gone to a certain nearby swamp and wetland preserve, an excellent spot to find a wide variety of woodpecker species. "No, I haven't," he replied. I then asked, "What areas around here *do* you find to be the best for bird-watching?" He seemed confused by the question, replying, "Oh, I've never gone bird-watching! I just like looking at pictures."

Granted that such photographs are wonderful, and granted that having an interest in them is better than having no interest in wildlife at all. But sitting in an easy chair poring over other people's bird pictures is no substitute for actually donning a pair of binoculars, getting out into the woods, and patiently seeking the genuine article. Merely viewing pictures is like adoring the sheet music for Beethoven's Fifth Symphony yet never hearing it performed by an orchestra. The sheet music may be nice — and it does contain the directions for performing the symphony — but looking at the score is by no means the same thing as experiencing a performance. Beethoven wrote the music to be performed, not merely to be read on paper!

It is only by tramping through the woods that you can not only see the colorful plumage of birds but also hear their songs, witness their sometimes comical behavior, and gain a sense for their natural habitats. People who only look at bird books or magazines have never seen the male cardinal tenderly feeding the female as part of their courtship ritual, have never witnessed the 70 miles per hour power dive of the peregrine falcon, have never heard the pure, liquid melody of the Swainson's thrush — a song so beautiful as to make tears leap to your eyes even as you sense God's own divine smile on a creature capable of such music.

The only way fully to delight in the creation is to get out into it. On weekends, Sunday afternoons, and certainly for more formal times of vacation, we should occasionally — if not routinely — seek out places where we can revel in the raw exuberance of this world. We often call our leisure time "recreation" — notice the word: re-*creation*. But where can we better re-create our spirits than in the original creation God made "in the beginning"?

In this connection we should also briefly take note of an excellent observation by Sallie McFague. McFague points out that there is such a thing as "environmental racism." By this she means that increasingly in our societies the poorest people are forced to live in the most polluted areas of the city. For instance, if a new waste incinerator is to be built, wealthier families can muster the political clout to keep it from being built in their backyards. The poor, on the other hand, have neither the political nor the financial resources to keep the incinerator from being built in their area; they also lack the money it would take to move away from this ugly source of pollution.

But as McFague notes, these same poor people lack the resources to travel out-of-state to national parks or other places of great natural beauty. It is for this reason Christians should support urban parks, including "pocket parks," which are little green areas planted and nurtured on just one or two vacant lots in the inner city. Although such parks are not a substitute for the true wonders of the larger world, they do provide our poorer citizens with at least some exposure to the wonders of creation and can, therefore, plant the seeds of "creation delight" into the hearts of many urban children and young people who would otherwise never see a tree, a bird, or a rabbit in the wild. [10]

A second set of suggestions related to the first is to find daily ways by which to educate ourselves and our children about the glories of creation. Today a variety of daily tear-off calendars are available from wildlife groups in local bookstores. Some of these feature a full-color photo of birds or other wildlife for each day, others give one fascinating fact or anecdote per day about plants, reefs, or other wildlife.

Although such secondhand facts and photos are no substitute for seeing the real thing, viewing a new picture or learning a curious fact each day can stoke the fires of our wonder even during those times when it is not feasible for us to get out of the house or city. Such daily learning and marveling can also whet our appetites for the genuine article even as it will enhance our experience once we do take a vacation or a weekend nature hike. Again, the more you know about the creation, the more you will get out of your experience in it. This may be especially true for children, who usually already possess a wide-eyed fascination with the creation. Giving them a daily opportunity to learn at least a little bit more about God's world may be one way for us to be good stewards of their God-given curiosity.

For all its faults cable and satellite television now offer us and our children new opportunities for education and revelry. The PBS show *Kratt's Creatures* is a delightful daily program that humorously entertains children even as it educates them about many kinds of animals from all over the world. It also delivers good, levelheaded messages on the need to preserve this wonderful world.

There are now similar programs available for all age levels, including whole networks (like the Discovery channel's Animal Planet station) devoted to nothing but educational programming about the natural world. In a time when many parents are waking up to the need to limit and control the amount and type of TV shows their children watch, Christian parents would do well to include these shows in a child's restricted television menu.

Third, if allergies and landlords permit, having a pet or a tropical fish aquarium can be a fun, loving way to bring something of the outside world inside. Every once in a while in the evening when our dog is curled up at our feet, my wife will comment that if you stop to think about it, it is rather strange to have an animal share your house with you. Although such pets are domesticated, they do bring a little something of the wider created world into our day-to-day lives. Pets are a tangible reminder that we are not alone on planet earth.

Frederick Buechner somewhere notes that if you look deeply into the eyes of animals like dogs, cats, and horses, you sense an intelligence and a capacity for feeling that, though by no means human, nevertheless speaks of our common Maker. When we recognize this in a pet, when we realize how we can come to love and grow attached to such animals in our homes, we may be reminded that all the creatures of this planet come from our loving God and that all of them are, therefore, worthy of our care, nurture, and protection. (Old Testament scholar Bernhard Anderson has pointed out that the fact that in Genesis 1 animals and humans are both made on the sixth day of creation is a subtle literary indication of the affinity between the nonhuman creation and human beings.) [11]

Being around animals reminds us there is good reason why Saint Francis of Assisi was forever calling birds and animals his "brothers and sisters." As theologian Francis Schaeffer pointed out, you do not need to subscribe to theories of evolution to recognize our link with all that exists. As Christians, we know we are ultimately related to jaguars and sugar maples simply because we were all made by the same Creator God. "The value of things is not in themselves autonomously, but that God made them — and thus they deserve to be treated with high respect. [So] when we meet an ant on the sidewalk, we step over him. He is a creature, like ourselves; not made in the image of God, but equal with man as far as creation is concerned. The ant and the man are both creatures." [12] Having pets in the house can remind us of this vital creation link and so can also inspire both our respect for all God's creatures and our praise of God for having made them all.

Fourth and finally we return to where we began the last chapter: in our churches. In his book *Earth-Wise* environmentalist Calvin DeWitt makes scores of good suggestions on how to make our congregations more eco-friendly and more celebrative of the creation. [13] In the next chapters we will ponder ways to protect and preserve the creation, but for now, highlighting our need to notice and delight in the creation, I will suggest some methods by which churches might lift up God's handiwork more often.

On the architectural side we could encourage a little retrofitting of our sanctuaries to make them more open to and reflective of the natural world. Whether this means having more windows, bringing in more plants and flowers, or finding other ways to symbolize and point to the creation, we should do what we can to make our contemporary houses of worship consistent with Solomon's temple and its artful ways of harking back to Eden. Perhaps banners, murals, and paintings could be used to remind worshipers that we do not come to God hermetically sealed behind brick and stained glass but worship him within the context of — and also with the help of — a stunning world of wonders.

Additionally, preachers and teachers should pay more attention to their own rhetorical use of the creation in sermons or lesson plans. In her book *Nature, God, and Pulpit* Elizabeth Achtemeier points out that once upon a time preachers — like the authors of the Bible — made much more frequent reference to the creation than they do now. In more agricultural settings and in more rural times, preachers often tried to draw their sermon illustrations from nature. Now, however, preachers are more likely to allude to TV shows, movies, and current events than they are to the natural world.

But as Achtemeier thoughtfully points out, if preachers are to be true to the Bible and to the God of the Bible, they must highlight the creation more often by using it as examples or as metaphors by which to make a point. This will also help congregations avoid the tendency to divorce God the Creator from God the Redeemer.

Similarly, in the larger liturgy those who choose hymns could work to include regularly, if not weekly, songs that point to and celebrate the creation. Many of the psalms do just this, and they also could be routinely sung, recited, or read as part of worship services. Those who pray in worship may also wish to keep concerns about God's world before them when pondering what to pray about on a given Sunday. On some weeks there may be specific wonders to give thanks for or specific disasters to be concerned about — perhaps the exuberance of autumn colors or the scent of fresh blossoms in the spring could be mentioned in praise; perhaps an oil spill or some new study on ozone depletion could be mentioned in a prayer for God's healing of these disasters and concerns.

In *The Screwtape Letters* C. S. Lewis imagines all the ways by which a demon might try to tempt a new Christian to sin — or at least to keep him from maturing too much in his newfound faith. In one of many poignant vignettes we see a senior devil advising a junior demon to make the new Christian always pray for the state of his mother's soul but never for something like her arthritis. The idea is to keep his prayers as "spiritual" as possible, thus removing the reality of God from the ordinary concerns of daily life. After all, if a Christian's prayers never address everyday things like arthritis or job performance, then his spirituality may eventually seem more like a separate little compartment off to the side of life instead of the all-encompassing, life-changing center to life that it should be.[14]

We face this temptation in our liturgical prayers in church. Bringing in the specifics of the creation — praising God for this world's beauty and pleading with God to heal its distressing decay — is one of many ways by which worship leaders and pastors can "connect" what happens on Sunday to the earthly reality of life Monday through Saturday. If in prayer we give thanks for the glorious dogwood tree just outside the church, the congregation's worship will continue as it leaves the building and gratefully takes note of this very same tree. If we pray for an oil slick off the Alaskan coast, members of the congregation may remember to do the same thing each time they read or hear about that spill in the week ahead.

Such prayers would heighten a congregation's overall awareness of the creation. Especially those who live in urban areas would do well to expand their prayer lives to include such concerns, for in city environments we tend to forget about things like crops, forests, and animals.

A couple of years ago at the annual meeting of my denomination, the delegates were presented with an innocent motion to move the denomination's annual day of prayer from early March to mid-May. Like most of my fellow delegates, I was prepared to vote on this without much thought. After all, I reasoned, what difference does it make when we pray?

But suddenly there was something of an uproar from the delegates who came from agricultural settings. Why were they upset? Because the annual day of prayer traditionally had been a key time to pray for the success of agriculture, including the sowing of the crops in springtime. "If you wait until May," one farmer pointed out, "it will be too late! Our crops will already be in the ground, and we would just as soon have you all pray for this *before* we do our planting!" He was right. Unhappily, those of us who live our lives in the city and get our food from huge supermarkets had no inkling of this possible objection. Once again we realized how easy it is — even in church — to live cut off from the concerns and rhythms of the natural world of God's creation.

In some church services we could expand our repertoire of praise by thanking God for the one creation wonder that is always inside our church sanctuaries: the human body! John Calvin once wrote that Christians should praise God for all of his manifold splendors, starting with the wonder of toenails, spleens, kidneys, and lungs. Throughout God's creation we find worlds within worlds, and the internal world of the human body is surely one of the most wondrous. Yet how often in church — or anywhere else — do we pause over the wonders that are inside our own skins? [15]

Ironically, compared with Calvin's day, we now know far more about the intricacies of the human body and so, by all rights, should have far more to praise God for. We could, for instance, marvel over and thank God for the miracle of DNA, allowing our minds to boggle over its complexity. For instance, printing out the standard names of the three billion base pairs of haploid genes within a single human person would require the number of pages in at least thirteen sets of the *Encyclopedia Britannica!* [16] The odds are that we have never heard a minister or liturgist thank God for internal organs or for our genetic codes, but perhaps it is high time we add such praises to our weekly worship practices. (Of course, we do regularly pray for people whose bodies are sick, but perhaps we would do well to give praise for bodies that are healthy and functioning well.)

We should encourage the members of our congregations to use Sunday as a day for reveling in the creation. In some traditions Sundays were once — and perhaps still are — dour, indoors-only days on which swimming, hiking, bike riding, and other outdoor activities were officially frowned upon as "breaking the Sabbath." Actually, a close look at the biblical notion of Sabbath may point us in quite another direction.

Of course, Christians technically do not observe the seventh day Sabbath (Saturday) as their weekly holy day but instead gather for worship on the first day of the week, the day of the resurrection: Sunday. Although there is some debate as to whether or to what extent the Christian Sunday should be regarded as the equivalent of the Jewish Sabbath, many Christians have nevertheless adopted the basic principles of Sabbath observance for use on Sundays. Principally the Bible tells us that on our weekly holy day there is to be no work. Instead it is a day of rest and worship.

Two primary biblical texts give instructions to Israel as to how they are to treat the Sabbath day: Exodus 20 and Deuteronomy 5, both of which present the Ten Commandments. However, a side by side study of these texts reveals a slight variation. When Exodus 20:11 tells Israel to observe a Sabbath day, it grounds this command in the creation: "For in six days the LORD made the heavens and the earth, the sea, and all that is in them, but he rested on the seventh day. Therefore the LORD blessed the Sabbath day and made it holy." In Deuteronomy 5:15, however, the reason given for the Sabbath is different. "Remember that you were slaves in Egypt and that the LORD your God brought you out of there with a mighty hand and an outstretched arm. Therefore the LORD your God has commanded you to observe the Sabbath day."

In other words, the Sabbath day's rest has a double focus: creation and redemption. On the one hand, it is a day to imitate God's own revelry in his creation. God's "rest" on the seventh day of creation was not the result of divine fatigue but of God's desire to enjoy what he had made, to watch it and smile over it and delight in it. On the other hand, Israel was to rest on the Sabbath day to give themselves a chance to remember the exodus from Egypt. They were not only to recall the time when they were never given a break by their cruel Egyptian taskmasters but also to remember how God had saved them from that life of wearisome misery. Part of Israel's grateful recollection of that salvation was to be symbolized by their giving themselves as well as their own servants and animals a day off.

Creation and redemption are the two great themes of all Scripture. Not surprisingly, they form the dual focus for the holy Sabbath day as well. Christians also would do well to make this twin Sabbath focus their own. Unhappily, it seems our Sundays now focus mostly on redemption but hardly at all on creation. So in addition to making the liturgical changes mentioned above, we should also encourage Christians to use their day of rest as a chance to take a Sunday afternoon tramp through the woods, to go to the beach and frolic in the surf, to spend some time in the backyard soaking up the sun or admiring the flowers and trees. The fourth commandment essentially tells us, "Remember creation!" Perhaps it is high time we Christians did just that on the Lord's day.

Beyond Sunday worship, we might also encourage our church's youth group and senior citizens club to plan excursions into the natural world. Instead of always going to amusement parks or miniature golf courses for their outings, young people could be exposed to various facets of God's creation by youth leaders providing appropriate guidance and education in these matters. So also coordinators of adult education programs could strive regularly to invite speakers who will hold seminars on the wonders of creation.

These and many issues like them are wholly appropriate for Christians to consider. For our God in Christ has redeemed this world and will one day renew the face of this creation. If it is true, as C. S. Lewis memorably wrote, that "joy will be the serious business of heaven," then it appears from the Bible that at least some of that heavenly joy will be the joy of mountains, lakes, streams, orchards, birds, fish.

If so, slivers of heavenly joy are already available to us today. At home with our children and friends, and certainly also in our houses of worship, we should educate ourselves to take notice of these slivers of heaven on earth — to notice and celebrate them with rejoicing.

On that Sunday the spider appeared on my pulpit Bible, I was startled and initially annoyed. I can now say I am glad that little guy dropped by. Metaphorically speaking, we Christians need to see spiders on our Bibles and in our churches far more often than we do.

Hearing Creation's Chorus

The Ecology of Praise I

Shaving the Planet

In C. S. Lewis's novel *That Hideous Strength* a demonic organization buys a parcel of ancient forest in England and proceeds immediately to clear-cut the forest's oldest and grandest trees. Some time later the leader of this group explains this action and tells of his ultimate, devilish plans for the world. "We seek the elimination of all real trees, replacing them with aluminum ones. I would also get rid of the birds. Consider the improvement: No feathers dropped about, no nests, no dirt. It's really simple hygiene: You shave your face, we shave the planet."[1]

Lewis's underlying idea is exactly right: God is the Creator of all things lovely and wonderful. But the devil despises the work of God's hands and so seeks to unmake it. Where the devil has his way, the lush richness of the creation's life is threatened, diminished, thinned down, hammered flat, and finally snuffed out.

God made a world bursting at the seams with swarms of life-forms, and God takes joy in each and every one of them — indeed, he has pronounced blessings over his many creatures. Perhaps nowhere in the Bible can these truths be better seen than in the more poetic books. By examining some of the psalms as well as poetic passages in the Book of Job, we again see the theme of God's divine delight over his creation. But in addition to making this creation delight our own, the Bible's revelation of God's love for his handiwork must inspire us to do all we can to care for and preserve this world of wonders in which we have been placed. If it is hypocritical, if not heretical, for Christians to live willingly cut off from the created order, it is surely also heretical to neglect that creation by allowing it to be plundered and polluted beyond recognition.

If we love God we will not only take an ardent interest in the work he produces but also treat that work with care and respect. It would be absurd to imagine a loving husband abusing his wife's art, callously throwing her paintings into the back of a closet, roughly handling a picture so that it is damaged, using one of her smaller paintings as a serving tray with which to bring drinks to some guests.

Is it not likewise absurd to imagine a person who believes this universe is the handiwork of God — carefully crafted by the divine Artisan — dumping chemicals into one of God's crystal clear rivers? Is it not also devastatingly unloving for us Christians to show little or no concern about the hunting of one of God's created species to extinction?

Many Christians today bristle with theological indignation when they hear someone suggest evolutionary processes, not God, brought about this cosmos. After all, we want to be clear that God, not happenstance, was supremely in charge of the process of creation. Occasionally, however, a Christian scientist will get into trouble by suggesting that even some of the species and life-forms on earth may have developed through a process of natural selection. Even if the scientist asserts this process was begun and superintended by God himself, many will deem this yet another attempt to put daylight between God and the process of creation. For many Christians, God must be in the details; his divine fingerprints must be on every distant quasar and on every subatomic quark.

Well and good. But why, then, are so many of these same Christians suspicious of — or at least apathetic toward — organizations that aim to preserve this world's welter of species? If we wish to resist the idea that God merely got the creation rolling once upon a time and let some species come about through mostly natural processes, and if we wish instead to insist on the up-close, personal attention with and by which God made all things, then we should have an even greater concern about river pollution, ozone depletion, and species extinctions.

After all, if we Christians really believe that it was God himself, and not merely the machinations of natural selection, who painted the lovely dappled colors onto the wings of a certain butterfly, then why would we ever support building a golf course over that butterfly's last remaining habitat? Would not our larger beliefs about God's detailed work of creation tell us that God pays special attention even to this butterfly? If we conclude that adding one more golf course to this world is more important than the survival of this unique butterfly, what is the difference between that action and a husband's callously puncturing a hole in one of his wife's prized paintings?

Calvin DeWitt uses a similar analogy to describe the church today. Imagine, DeWitt says, that one day you discover a Rembrandt Appreciation Society in your city. You find out this is a group of people who love to get together to discuss the artistry of Rembrandt's paintings, praising the artist, toasting his genius, and marveling over his skill. Then imagine your shock if you discovered that this society rarely if ever goes to museums to see the actual paintings and is wholly unperturbed to hear that one of Rembrandt's famous paintings had been stolen or that *The Nightwatch* had been viciously slashed by art-hating thugs. Suppose one of the society's members says, "Oh, that doesn't matter. The main thing is that we remember who Rembrandt is, regardless of what happens to his work!"[2]

Surely this would widen the eyes. But, DeWitt asks, what is the difference between this fictional society and the church? How can we praise the Creator for his work each week but never go to see it? How can we so ardently defend the detailed work of God against even the mildest of evolutionists and yet not bat an eye when one of those detailed works of God winks out of existence?

God did indeed make the wonders we see around us in this cosmos. He takes a joyful, playful delight in these wonders — a joy we would do well to cultivate in our own lives. But the Bible gives us still more reasons to be concerned about God's world. The Bible reveals that this universe praises God no less than we human beings do when we gather in our churches to sing hymns. This is a praise chorus God surely wishes to preserve.

This is what I call "the ecology of praise" — creation's choir that sings a song of high and holy praise to God's name. But this very chorus is what makes the devil so interested in spoiling the creation. The glorious singing of the cosmos grates on the devil's ears for the same reason a lovely choral anthem by Bach infuriates him. All hymns of praise to God, no matter who sings or produces them, are despised by those who oppose the Creator and Redeemer God. But it is for this reason the followers of God must care for and preserve the creation's chorus.

As we approach the end of the twentieth century and of the second millennium, the need to be preservers of creation's choir has gained a high profile and a new urgency. Although the scientific data are a matter of fierce debate and unending controversy, few could plausibly deny we are now surrounded by indicators of decay. Globally there is reason for concern in the thinning of the ozone layer, in the increase of trapped atmospheric gases like carbon dioxide, in the steady decline of the rain forests and the slow but sure dying of coral reefs.

Even those who question the urgency of these planetwide problems cannot deny that many local communities face dire threats to the health and safety of all life-forms. In the Third World, mind-numbing numbers of people and other creatures die because of polluted water supplies; some estimate nearly four million people die each year. Many children in the world today have no access to a clean cup of water or an uncontaminated fish. Others in more industrialized nations live near contaminated soil where vegetables can no longer be grown or safely eaten.

As I write this in the fall of 1997, I reflect on several news stories. Fish along parts of the east coast of the United States are suffering from a flesh-eating disease scientists believe is caused by bacteria that feed on certain forms of pollution in the water. A newspaper report stated that more of Brazil's rain forests are on fire right now than at any time in history as farmers burn vast parcels of forest to make room for cattle pastures. At an international conference on global warming, scientists again presented evidence of increasing temperatures worldwide — a trend that, were it to continue unchecked, could have devastating consequences.

In the Pacific northwest many farmers can no longer use their land because of a toxic buildup of heavy metals. Shockingly, these metals, unbeknownst to the farmers, had been put in the fertilizers they had been using for years. These substances — including mercury and lead — were ingredients in the fertilizers neither because they helped plants grow nor by accident but because, it was revealed, fertilizer manufacturers had been paid by other corporations to take these toxic wastes off their hands. Although each bag or tank of fertilizer contained a safe amount of these waste products, over time the toxic metals built up in the soil, finally reaching anything but safe amounts.

Unhappily, it seems almost every environmental statistic is susceptible to manipulation both by those who wish to make the crisis appear more dire and by those who wish to minimize it. Even among books by Christian authors there are frequently fierce disagreements. Books like Calvin College's *Earthkeeping in the Nineties* and Calvin DeWitt's *Earth-Wise,* as well as publications by organizations like the Christian Society of the Green Cross, highlight many of the ecological concerns mentioned above. Meanwhile two recent books from the Acton Institute — *The Cross and the Rain Forest* and E. Calvin Beisner's *Where Garden Meets Wilderness* — accuse evangelical scholars of utilizing "junk science" to create fears and concerns in the Christian community.

But as is often the case in such situations, even if the truth lies somewhere in between, God's creation is still in trouble in ways that have seldom before been true. Yes, critics of the environmentalist movement are right to point out there is also good news to report; we have made gains in the last fifty years in curtailing some forms of pollution, in increasing recycling, in helping many endangered species thrive once again. And there is evidence that despite all our rough handling of the earth, the planet appears to be remarkably resilient. At least some of the threats we now face may be counterbalanced by other phenomena on the planet.

However, none of that means — as some Christian authors appear to believe — that the ecological crisis is a fiction. None of that means we can relax, allowing our massively acquisitive consumer culture to go unchecked. On the other hand, Christians need not be frightened into environmental paralysis. Christians, of all people, have reason for hope, reason to believe that the Creator remains invested in the work of his hands and that this same God has endowed us, who bear his image, with the ability to carry out our stewardly task even in a time of increased threats and decay.

If it is true that the devil would love to spoil the creation — to "shave the planet" of the lush richness God has caused to grow on the face of the earth — we nevertheless have reason for hope. For we know that the devil is a vanquished foe — none of his plans or ambitions will ever come to fruition. For Christians, therefore, the struggle to preserve God's creation is carried out with confidence, with zestful hope, and in the power of God's Holy Spirit, who personally seals Christ's victory over all evil right into our very hearts.

A Cosmic Coat of Many Colors

O LORD my God, you are very great; you are clothed with splendor and majesty.
He wraps himself in light as with a garment; he stretches out the heavens like a tent.

How many are your works, O LORD! In wisdom you made them all; the earth
is full of your creatures.

Psalm 104:1–2, 24

Above and beyond any specific threats to the creation, however, we need to ponder why Christians should esteem this universe in the first place. Why are Christians properly invested in this world and why should they also, therefore, work diligently to promote its preservation? Just what is this universe and how is it related to our almighty God? These days, as has been true throughout history, there are quite a few answers to those questions, some of which accord quite readily with the Bible and some of which clearly cut against the grain of Scripture. So before we probe too deeply into various reasons why we should preserve this creation, we would do well to establish clearly just what the Bible reveals to be the nature of this creation and its relationship to God.

Old Testament scholar John Stek refers to the cosmos as "the glory robe of God," a phrase nicely suggested by Psalm 104. Such an image helps us avoid a couple of common pitfalls to which many people fall prey today. Above all else we wish to affirm the traditional theological tenet that the Creator and the creation are distinct. Any teaching that blurs the lines between God and creation runs the risk of idolatry — the sin of calling any nondivine thing or person "God" and then worshiping that object accordingly. Two current yet very old teachings that promote such idolatry are pantheism and panentheism.

Pantheism teaches that the entire cosmos is identical with God — the universe just *is* divine. These days pantheism is making a comeback among New Age devotees — indeed, numerous home pages on pantheism can be found on the World Wide Web. But this teaching can also be detected among those who hold to ideas such as the religious version of the Gaia hypothesis.

In scientific terms the Gaia hypothesis asserts that the earth has a remarkable ability to maintain a level of equilibrium on a global scale. For instance, the salinity (salt content) of the oceans remains steady at 3.4 percent (were this percentage even a little higher, marine life would die on a massive scale). The total volume of water on earth has remained constant for aeons. The level of oxygen in the atmosphere has from time immemorial been 21 percent (again, were there only a little more oxygen in our air — say about 25 percent — the earth would become a fireball).

So the scientific version of Gaia merely traces the earth's remarkable ability to maintain all of these vital elements in exact balance. There is, however, also a religious version of Gaia, which posits that the reason the earth can pull off this delicate balancing act is because the entire planet is itself a living, breathing, feeling being all its own — a being that is just possibly divine.

For Christians, however, any pantheistic teaching that declares the earth or the universe divine is regarded as idolatrous and in violation of the key biblical injunction to "worship the Lord God and him only." (Christians should, however, appreciate the scientific version of Gaia. After all, biblically informed Christians have a name for this planet's astonishing self-adjusting abilities: divine providence!) [3]

A teaching more subtle than pantheism is panentheism, which posits that although God and the cosmos are not completely identical, God — or at least portions of God's being — can be found within the natural world. As such, panentheists claim that the universe is at least an extension of God. Even a Christian theologian like Sallie McFague may be propounding a panentheistic idea when she calls the cosmos the "body of God." McFague claims this is only a metaphor or working model and should not be taken as a literal description. Still, we must choose even our metaphors carefully. In this case it may be that the difference between God and the idea of God's "body" may not be stark enough to avoid an idolatrous identifying of God with the physical world.[4]

By way of analogy, consider how we regard our own bodies. Granted that Christians believe human beings are more than just bodies; we believe we have a soul or spirit that will survive the death of our bodies. At the same time, however, we identify closely with our bodies; we cannot think of ourselves without thinking also of our bodies. Hence, a woman who is raped would never claim that the attack need not affect her spirit since it was, after all, something that touched only her body. (Indeed, her body's scars will heal far more quickly and efficiently than will her soul's.) Similarly, but more positively, if a lover tenderly holds your hand, the meaning of that gesture goes far beyond the mere physical warmth of flesh on flesh; it touches and warms also your heart.

Being an embodied spirit is essential to our humanity — so much so that the Bible promises an embodied existence even in the eternity of God's kingdom. So if we picture the universe being to God what skin and bones are to a human being, we would be forced to admit that everything is sacred in the same way that God is sacred. Even as a metaphor, calling the cosmos God's body leads one to imagine God's identifying with this world in a way similar to how we identify with our bodies. In that case it is a short leap to saying that our bowing before and touching an oak tree would be a way to bow before and worship God. Touch my hand and you touch me; touch God's world and you touch God.

But this amounts to a subtle form of idolatry the Bible is everywhere exceedingly careful to avoid. Unlike the fertility religions of Canaan, Babylon, and other surrounding cultures, ancient Israel refused to identify the earth, the sky, the rain, or anything else as part of God. Creator and creation are distinct. God is spirit and is to be worshiped as such — so much so that the Israelites were forbidden to make any kind of visual image, painting, statue, totem, or mosaic that depicts God.

So rather than import the metaphor of a body, we should stick with the biblical metaphor of the universe as God's glory robe, which he wraps around himself in splendor and might. This is a garment that God himself fashioned and that is utterly dear to him, but this robe of splendor is not the same thing as God.

Of course, those who call the entire universe divine and those who, like McFague, try to elevate the importance of the universe by calling it God's body often have noble goals. Such writers desire to engender greater respect for the world; they wish to make us see how dear the cosmos is to God so that we might treat it accordingly. For McFague, if metaphorically we see the earth as part of God's very body, we will tread lightly on that earth in the same way we hope others will treat our own bodies with tenderness and respect.

But we need not go to these lengths to find reasons to uphold the creation. For the Bible makes clear that the cosmos does reveal God's own glory. The universe is not divine, but it is transparent to its divine Maker; it is his resplendent garment that is itself a visible manifestation of his splendor. What is more, this glory robe is a living garment that praises God in ways utterly pleasing to the Creator.

Creation's Chorus

> The heavens declare the glory of God; the skies proclaim the work of his hands. Day after day they pour forth speech; night after night they display knowledge. There is no speech or language where their voice is not heard.
>
> Psalm 19:1–3

> Praise the LORD.... Praise him, sun and moon, praise him, all you shining stars.... Praise the LORD from the earth, you great sea creatures and all ocean depths, lightning and hail, snow and clouds, stormy winds that do his bidding, you mountains and all hills, fruit trees and cedars, wild animals and all cattle, small creatures and flying birds, kings of the earth and all nations, you princes and all rulers on earth, young men and maidens, old men and children. Let them praise the name of the LORD, for his name alone is exalted; his splendor is above the earth and the heavens.
>
> Psalm 148:1, 3, 7–12

The universe witnesses to its Maker in speech more elegant than the finest human words — more wonderfully than even the eloquent poetry of the Bible's psalms. In Psalm 19 we are told that the universe preaches and proclaims the glory of God and that it does so incessantly. But, of course, you have to listen well to hear it.

In a memorable sermon, Frederick Buechner once pondered what would happen if, one night, God changed the order of the stars so they spelled "I Exist." Buechner claims if such a thing were to happen, there probably would be a great turning toward God. Churches would fill up, agnostics would become believers, atheists would be shaken.

But after a while the novelty would wear off. Scientists would explain the phenomenon naturalistically. Philosophers would debate to whom *I* referred. Linguists would analyze the verb *exist* until no one was sure what it meant, either. Atheists would eventually claim they saw nothing whatsoever in the night sky — it's just a bunch of stars; so what? The words "I Exist" eventually would become just another constellation in the night sky, making no more of an impression than does the Big Dipper. [5]

Buechner's point is that you need a special set of eyes to behold the presence of our loving Creator God. In fact, although the words "I Exist" do not appear in the stars of the night sky or anywhere else, the eye of faith nevertheless essentially sees these words everywhere. In the design painted on the shell of a turtle, in the spouting of whales, in the song of the eastern meadowlark, and in a billion other such ways, the words "I Exist" are there for the reading. For the universe witnesses to God.

But the true wonder of the psalms and other similar biblical passages is the revelation that the universe also praises God. We are told that birds sing to God, that trees clap their hands to God, that rivers leap to praise God. We mostly chalk this up as mere metaphor. Such sentiments, we believe, are not to be taken literally. When a poet describes his lover as a red, red rose, we don't expect this woman to be made out of a green stem with petals for a face. When Shakespeare asks in a sonnet, "Shall I compare thee to a summer's day?" we don't expect the woman in question actually to resemble sunlight, breezes, and fluffy clouds.

So when the psalmists tell us the universe "sings" or "speaks of" God's glory, well, that's just poetry. After all, we are not to think that cardinals actually whistle their clarion melodies for God, are we? We are not to think that crickets rub their legs together to lift up the name of God, are we? We are not to place the haunting songs of humpback whales on a par with a Christian congregation's singing "Praise God, from Whom All Blessings Flow," are we? Surely this is just poetic license — metaphors not to be taken literally.

Yet from the Bible it appears that we are indeed to take this literally. Psalm 148 is called an "imperative hymn" by scholars. The first and last words of the psalm are the Hebrew words *hallelu yah*. In our English use of the word *Hallelujah!* we typically use this Hebrew phrase as a personal statement of praise, as the equivalent of our saying, "I am now thanking you, O God." But in the original Hebrew *hallelu yah* is actually neither a simple indicative statement nor an exclamatory outburst but an imperative statement that orders others to join the chorus of cosmic praise to God. So when the psalmists begin or close their poems with *Hal-*

lelujah — now often translated "Praise the LORD" — they are not making a statement but are issuing an order for the whole world to join them in singing to God. It is the psalmist's way of pointing his finger and shouting, "Hey, you over there — join the chorus and praise God along with me right now!"

Psalm 148 is one of many poems in the Hebrew Psalter that is an extended command to sing to God. This is the cosmic praise imperative. Curiously, however, in Psalm 148 human beings are mentioned dead last in this litany. Long before the psalmist gets around to our human need to praise God, he focuses first on how the moon, stars, whales, winds, mountains, apple trees, Scottish terriers, crickets, and hummingbirds sing to God. The whole creation exists to praise God, the psalmist is telling us. Yes, people who sing in church choirs or who lift up their voices in a hymn praise God, but so do the sun and the snow. Yes, it makes sense to give this praise imperative to human beings, but it makes equal sense to this psalmist to speak to the rest of the creation as well. The psalmist makes no differentiation between his words to the hail and his words to maidens and old men. There is nothing in Psalm 148 that indicates that the words about whales praising God are metaphorical whereas the words about kings and young men praising God are literal.

So perhaps all this *is* meant literally. Perhaps in God's ears, all of this world's sounds really are songs of praise — and what a chorus it is! Some time ago an ornithologist observed a single red-eyed vireo singing its song 22,197 times in a single day! Conservative estimates say that in North America alone there are as many as six billion land birds. So let us be conservative and say that on a given day in the season of spring — the time of the year when birds tend to sing the most — each of these birds sings its song about ten thousand times. That would be, in North America alone, sixty trillion songs in just one day. "Day after day they pour forth speech." Indeed they do, and God is listening.

Of Storks and Hippos

> The trees of the LORD are well watered, the cedars of Lebanon that he planted. There the birds make their nests; the stork has its home in the pine trees. The high mountains belong to the wild goats; the crags are a refuge for the coneys.
>
> There is the sea, vast and spacious, teeming with creatures beyond number.... There the ships go to and fro, and the leviathan, which you formed to frolic there.
>
> Psalm 104:16-18, 25–26

"Do you know when the mountain goats give birth? Do you watch when the doe bears her fawn?"

"The wings of the ostrich flap joyfully, but they cannot compare with the pinions and feathers of the stork."

"Look at the behemoth [hippopotamus], which I made along with you.... He ranks first among the works of God.... The hills bring him their produce, and all the wild animals play nearby."

Job 39:1, 13; 40:15, 19a, 20

God delights in this world's symphony of praise. Indeed, God delights in all the creatures he has made. C. S. Lewis once noted that in the Hebrew Psalter — and in the Bible generally — you find something found almost nowhere else in world literature. Again and again the Bible praises God for creatures unconnected to human beings. It is one thing to thank God for cows who produce milk for us or for plants that produce succulent fruit. But the psalmists do not stop there.

Psalm 104 praises God also for trees where storks nest, for rocky crags where eagles roost, for nooks where coneys live, for mountain peaks where wild goats frolic. In the Book of Job, God highlights his own glory by pointing to, of all things, the hippopotamus. Hippos don't do anything for humans. We don't eat them, we don't plow fields with them, we don't use their hides for clothing. No, hippos exist for the sheer joy and entertainment of the Creator.[6]

Earlier I suggested that when God "rested" on the seventh day, he kicked back to revel in all that he had made. You see a little of this same divine revelry emerging in Psalm 104:26 when God speaks delightfully about his watching the playful antics of whales; indeed, this is one of only two places in the entire Bible where the word *frolic* appears, the other being Jeremiah 50:11, which refers to a heifer that frolics as it threshes grain. The Bible in the psalms, and especially at the end of the Book of Job, tells us God gets a kick out of watching hawks soar, whales swim, ostriches flap their wings, deer give birth to wobbly-legged fawns, and great, galumphing hippos wade through rivers.

The animals of this world are not only loved *by* God, they also show love *to* God by declaring his praises. In this light we can understand why in the Bible God shows such a consistent concern for animals. Of course, there can be little debate that humankind has preeminence in Scripture. Although some environmentalists would have us place animals and humans on a par — some go so far as to place human beings below animals in importance — we would have to stretch things to make a scriptural case for such a move. Animals are not of equal value to human beings, nor certainly are they to be reckoned as having higher value. Throughout Scripture we are warned not to worship animals — neither living animals nor carved images of them. Animals are our fellow creatures, but they are also available for human beings to eat, to use in plowing fields, or to ride for transportation.

This is not to say, however, that God has no concern for animals. In Genesis, before he deluged the world with the great flood, God first contracted with Noah to build a huge ark, only a small portion of which was dedicated to saving Noah and his family. The vast majority of the ark's bulk was needed to preserve God's beloved animals and birds. It is thus unsurprising — albeit highly striking — that after the flood, when God makes his rainbow covenant with Noah, God makes abundantly clear that this covenant was also being made with the nonhuman creation. "Then God said to Noah and to his sons with him, 'I now establish my covenant with you and with your descendants after you *and with every living creature that was with you*'" (Gen. 9:8–10, emphasis added). One of the most vital aspects of biblical theology is the idea of covenant. How striking it is to see, therefore, that one of God's first biblical covenants was made not only with humanity but also with the animals and birds.

A similar divine concern for animals emerges at the end of the Book of Jonah. When God explained to Jonah why he delighted in not destroying the city of Nineveh, he stated that there were 120,000 people in that great city "and many cattle as well." This last item seems a strange addition to God's reasoning, unless we recognize what was stated above: God is tender and compassionate in his care for *all* the creatures of his hand.

In his book *The Way of Jesus Christ* German theologian Jürgen Moltmann highlights the Bible's presentation of God's concern for nonhuman creatures.[7] Moltmann believes that some of the best hints regarding God's attitude toward his creation can be found in some of those rather obscure Old Testament laws in Leviticus and Deuteronomy. For there it is curious to note that in Sabbath day regulations God always includes the animals. No one is to work on the Sabbath, including oxen, donkeys, and cows.

God's purposes in instituting the Sabbath observance are manifold, but among them is this: that the people of God might enter into the rhythm of creation. The Sabbath is a day to thank God for all that he has made and to thank him for saving us from our sins. For this reason the Sabbath has traditionally been a time for worship, a time to reflect upon Yahweh and our utter reliance on him. But if all of that is true, why might it be important that animals — who presumably know and can do none of this — also enter in to that rest?

Even more odd, in God's regulations regarding the seventh year sabbatical, God also orders that the land be given a Sabbath year rest. This regulation stretches matters further still. Why would God be concerned to give inert soil a break? Why give a rest to something that presumably does not know fatigue in the first place?

In the past we have seen these commandments as relating primarily to human beings. It is not so important that the land rest but that the land not be cultivated in order to insure that people rest. It is not so important that oxen and camels have one day off a week, but by mentioning them, God goes one step further to insure that people will also take the day off.

Yet perhaps we can and should do more with these passages than we traditionally have. Perhaps we need to see behind these regulations a fatherly concern for the environment proper. God upholds land and animals with his tender hand. God is concerned about animals. Yes, human beings are of greater importance. Yes, animals can be eaten, sacrificed, and worked for human benefit. But no, they are not insignificant in God's sight.

As Moltmann puts it, the Sabbath is the day of rest for the whole of God's community — animals included. The Sabbath is a day of reflection on creation. It is the day to respect God's handiwork. This includes animals and land and all else that has come from God and that God once declared "very good."

In recent years a fairly vigorous debate has been waged among ethicists and scholars as to whether it is appropriate to speak of "animal rights." On the more philosophical end of the spectrum are those who claim that granting someone rights always implies that the being in question can also fulfill certain moral duties. Having rights implies having the ability to fulfill obligations, and since animals have no duties and no moral sense, we cannot meaningfully grant them rights in a way similar to how we grant human beings rights. On the less heady end of the debate spectrum, however, are those who point out that simply possessing life — a life that Christians believe is ultimately granted by God himself — is itself a sufficient reason for recognizing that any living creature has a "right" to be respected and handled with care.

But perhaps we need not get into the intricacies of human rights versus animal rights. Perhaps we can engender respect and love for our fellow creatures simply by recognizing that all life comes from God and that God takes great delight in all his creatures, including those that have no connection to humanity.

It is for this reason that Joseph Kirwan's perspective on animals, as presented in the book *The Cross and the Rainforest,* is so woefully inadequate. Kirwan declares unequivocally that "the animal rights movement is pagan. Its advocates give no credence to ... the gulf which lies between man and the merely natural world." [8] But for a Christian there is no such thing as "the merely natural world." For biblically informed Christians there is only God's creation to consider. Kirwan and his coauthors appear never to ponder the divine perspective on this world, opting instead again and again to take only human needs, human wants, and human perspectives into account. Hence Kirwan approvingly quotes from writer Tibor Machen, who claims, "If man were uniquely important, that would mean that one could not assign any value to plants or non-humans *apart from their relationship to human beings*" (emphasis added). [9] A bit later Kirwan sums up his argument by saying, "Dominion of man over man is licit only when it is for the common good, that is, a good which both orderer and ordered share. The case of man's dominion over creatures is different. The dominator of an animal only has to consider human good." [10]

While it is true that humans are indeed unique in bearing God's divine image, it is not for that reason true that we regard the creation only in terms of its human utility or of its relationship to us. For Christians it is wholly proper to remember that God has his own view of this world and of its many creatures. God goes so far as to say, "Look at the hippopotamus *which I made along with you.* He ranks *first* among the works of God" (Job 40:15, 19a, emphases added). Any discussion on animals that fails to take into account the divine gaze is dreadfully out of sync with the Bible's own revelation regarding nonhuman creatures.

One need not degrade the importance of humanity — as some animal rights activists clearly do — to recognize the inherent value of animals above and beyond human utility. Earlier in *The Cross and the Rainforest* Kirwan's coauthor, Robert Whelan, hints ominously of the mayhem that can come if one esteems animals too much when he points out that the Nazis were staunch environmentalists, even going so far as to outlaw scientific experiments on animals as well as other forms of animal cruelty. Since these same Nazis went on to exterminate about six million human beings, Whelan's analogy would appear to be that if you love animals too much, you may inevitably hate humanity so much that you kill humans! [11] (Of course, Hitler was also a social conservative who eschewed alcohol, tobacco, and foul language. But that hardly means that all of the teetotaling, nonsmoking, morally upright Christians in America's Bible Belt are teetering on the brink of fostering genocide!)

In Old Testament Sabbath regulations as well as in passages from the psalms and the Book of Job, we discern a hint of God's divine concern for all he has made. If God desires that inert land and "ignorant" animals likewise enter into his Sabbath rest, then that places a value on creation that goes beyond what we have traditionally thought. If God is constantly looking at and enjoying the creatures he has made, then our human perspectives on animals can never be the final word on the subject; we can only stop our reflections on how we treat this world's creatures after we have thoroughly taken into account the divine perspective. "The earth is the Lord's, and everything in it," writes the poet of the 24th psalm. We would do well to remember that.

For ultimately all of these biblical streams of thought finally merge into the mighty river we are calling the ecology of praise. Consider: if the welter of this world's many and varied creatures exists to delight and to praise God, then as these creatures are diminished both in numbers and variety, God's praise is also diminished. And who wants to see the chorus of God's praise shrink more than the devil?

Let There Be Silence?

As we saw earlier, savvy writers like C. S. Lewis have picked up on this idea and have depicted a devil who would love to see a world without real trees and real birds. Some years ago environmentalist-author Rachel Carson wrote a landmark work on the environmental crisis — indeed, some credit Carson with beginning the modern ecological movement. She titled her book *Silent Spring*, pondering through her title if pollution and development might some day lead to a spring in which no warblers would sing, no trees would clack their branches together, no geese would honk. The devil would love such a silent spring. But it would break God's heart.

This divine heartbreak has been depicted by other writers as well; in fact, such demonic wrecking of the creation is a motif or recurring theme in literature, presenting the devil as a spoiler of creation. In the film version of John Updike's novel *The Witches of Eastwick* Jack Nicholson fiendishly plays the role of a devil who moves into a small New England town. He quickly proceeds to build a huge estate on a sensitive wetland that has long been the local home of the snowy egret. Later in the film this devil strolls around with a pair of binoculars, wickedly grinning as he asks, "Have you seen any egrets? I can't seem to find any egrets anymore!"

In John Milton's *Paradise Lost* the demons decide that if they cannot possess this world, they will do their best to smudge and sear it. What better way to hurt God than to harm what he holds dear? Other literary works show demons being hurt by anything that is bright or light. For theirs is a dark, dim, and dank realm, and their goal is to turn the whole cosmos back into chaos.

Perhaps the single most vivid portrayal of such a horrible demonic realm is Dante's classic *The Inferno*. The devil's realm reeks of sulphur and decay; it is devoid of light, color, heat, and life of any kind. It is the realm of the dead — a place where praise of God withers along with the life of God's creation.

Similarly, in J. R. R. Tolkien's popular *Lord of the Rings* trilogy the realm of evil is the land called Mordor. But unlike the bright, grassy, sunny parts of Tolkien's fictional world of Middle Earth, Mordor is a slaggy, gray, burnt-over region of belching volcanoes, cloudy skies, and tangible evil.

Where evil has its way, the lushness of creation is diminished, whittled away, and ultimately obscured from view. Such hellish visions can even be seen right here on earth whenever a major war is fought. Some time ago my wife and I were watching a documentary about World War I. At one point we noticed that in all of the photos and films of the battlefields in France and Germany, the landscape had become barren because of the barrage of artillery, grenades, and mortars. The once-beautiful Ardennes Forest in France had become shattered, the trees stripped of leaves or toppled to the ground, the once-green fields reduced to muddy tank tracks, the light of the sun obscured by clouds of acrid smoke.

As technology makes our weapons of war more efficient destroyers, the evil of war becomes an ever better spoiler of not only human life but of all life. One day in 1918, near the end of World War I, 2,700 artillery guns opened fire along the Allied front. At a cost of $1 million per minute, the guns continued to fire for three straight hours. In those three hours alone, the Allies expended more ammunition than had been used during the entire course of the American Civil War. The barrage snuffed out thousands of human lives and also laid waste to a huge region of the earth. [12]

Today's nuclear weapons carry still more potential for global destruction, but so do incendiary weapons like napalm and white phosphorous. Some of us can remember news footage that showed whole segments of Vietnam's lush jungles disappearing in a hellish orange napalm fireball. Munitions experts tell us that the chemical ingredients used in these weapons will continue to burn everything they touch until there is nothing left to burn.

War, the weapons of war, and the resulting destruction of all life in its path can delight only one set of beings in the cosmos: the devil and his hosts. As Christian stewards, we must abhor all such demonic havoc — havoc that continues with or without the raging of a war. For those with eyes to see, the burning over, flattening out, dirtying up, and wanton depleting of this world and its variety of creatures is something that is happening every day. This is a juggernaut of destruction that we must try to halt, or at least slow down.

However, not everyone agrees that our planet is facing unprecedented pollution and diminishment. Among scientists and politicians, fierce debates are waged as to whether this planet really is heating up. Still others question whether it is true that species are going extinct any faster today than at any other time in history. Thus, some doubt the wisdom of laws aimed to cordon off certain lands from development or to preserve a given species. Perhaps, some say, this is too much fuss and effort for too small a crisis.

I will not attempt to untie these various science and policy knots. Instead I wish to suggest a biblical starting point and overall direction for our thoughts in these matters. Specific questions of science and the environment need to be faced and weighed individually, prudently taking into account all of the data that bears on any particular question. Still, if we are to be biblically and theologically informed Christians, we should sort out every issue within a consistent framework. Each issue may be different, but our approach, goals, and ultimate decisions should be informed by the same set of criteria every time.

As Christians we must be caretakers of this world regardless of how any given debate on the nature of pollution turns out. Suppose someone could prove that the environmental crisis is not as bad as some have been claiming the last thirty or forty years. Suppose someone could decisively demonstrate that global warming and ozone depletion are not the major threats some scientists have asserted. Or suppose someone could prove through fossil records that it is simply unavoidable that a certain number of species will regularly go extinct.

Even if any or all of this could be proven — unlikely, given the complexity of most of these issues — it would not change how Christians should view and treat the world. The reason is that we would still be obligated to nurture this world and do all we can to preserve its beauty, its creatures, and its lush variety of life-forms. Unhappily, some who discount certain theories or softpedal current threats to the environment do so to tell people simply to relax. There is little or no need for us to change our lifestyles or habits since things are going along pretty smoothly anyway. The earth will take care of itself.

That attitude, however, is wrong. We must be self-conscious earthkeepers and caretakers, doing whatever we can to minimize pollution, animal suffering, and habitat destruction worldwide.

Why? What is our relationship to this world and to whom are we ultimately accountable in that relationship? These are questions we must answer before we can even begin to sketch out any specific suggestions as to how we should preserve and care for this cosmos.

So now we will consider the place of humanity in God's larger ordering of the universe, being careful to avoid the extremes either of degrading humanity's importance or of over-elevating our needs and wants to the point that we measure our actions only according to what we humans want or need.

Bearing God's Image
in the Creation

The Ecology of Praise 2

Masters or Servants?

A few years ago *Time* magazine writer Charles Krauthammer wrote an essay titled "Saving Nature, but Only for Man." In it he claimed we need to stop pollution simply because it is in our own best interests to do so. After all, let the ozone layer get depleted and we will eventually all be walking melanomas. Let corporations belch out smoke willy-nilly and we will all eventually have black lungs.

But Krauthammer also said we should not be too quick to preserve species if their demise is necessary to benefit human beings. If some caribou in Alaska need to die so we can get at some more oil, so be it. We need the oil and shouldn't have to fight with Middle Eastern Arabs to get at it. Spotted owls are nice, but loggers must live, so let them buzz through trees at will. Krauthammer claimed that the only environmentalism that will win wide support is one that admits right up front that nature is here to serve humanity, not the other way around. [1]

But for Christians this approach will never do. Still, some Christians present precisely this same point of view. According to Robert Sirico, "Nature does not have a metaphysical right ... to be preserved and adored for reasons other than its usefulness to God's human creatures." [2] This perspective, however, is every bit as narrow and wantonly anthropocentric as Christianity's harshest critics have ever claimed. It further short-circuits the biblical revelation that God has his own perspective of delight and joy in creation that we must always consider when discussing matters relating to the creation. The creation's usefulness to humanity is not the end of the matter; God's wishes for how we are to act as his designated vice-regents must be the final consideration.

For the Bible declares that we humans are here first of all to serve God and to attend to his world in ways reminiscent of God himself. Contrary to Krauthammer and Sirico, therefore, we must insist nature is not our servant; we are nature's servants. However, if a human-centered approach represents one extreme — making humanity and its needs the first and final arbiter in decisions on pollution levels or the survival of a given species — then the other extreme is surely also wrong.

For there are certain radical strains of ecological teaching that claim humanity is so detrimental to this planet — and so unnecessary to the flourishing of the nonhuman inhabitants of this world — it would be well if humanity as a whole were wiped from the face of the earth. Adherents of the Deep Ecology movement frequently make ludicrous claims about the status of humanity, some going so far as to label humans themselves as "pollutants" of the earth while others celebrate the AIDS virus and African famines because they result in fewer people on the planet![3] According to these environmentalist radicals, human beings are not superior to other creatures but are in fact inferior — so much so that we should volunteer to take ourselves out of the picture as a service to the other species of the planet!

This is an admittedly bizarre fringe of the larger ecological movement. However, sometimes faint echoes of these ideas can be heard even in the teachings of some Christian theologians. In her book *The Body of God* theologian Sallie McFague feels that the "common creation story" as taught to us by science — that is, the larger story of a billions-year-old universe that has evolved over time — must now take precedence over the "Genesis myth," which she claims no longer functions as a working model by which people can make sense of life.[4]

Instead, the common creation story teaches us to see ourselves as just one of the many by-products of a long evolutionary history. We must see and appreciate our link to all else that exists and thus treat all other creatures as distant (and sometimes not so distant) cousins. Thus, McFague claims, "One of the most critical house rules [of this planet] we must learn is that we are not lords over the planet, but products of its processes."[5] It is to help us recognize our link with all that surrounds us and to motivate us to care for this universe that McFague introduces her nonbiblical image of the cosmos as "the body of God."

McFague is not alone. A good many Christian writers today are suggesting similar views of humanity. In his book *Redeeming the Time,* Stephen Bede Scharper summarizes a number of recent works of Christian ecology. Scharper's survey of this literature makes clear that many Christian writers are now searching for new ways to define humanity's relationship with the nonhuman world, usually dumping all notions of human superiority or dominance in favor of proposing coequal relationships of mutuality between humans and nonhumans. Clearly, many Christians have concluded that setting humanity apart as special is too risky. Since this "anthropocentric" approach has led to environmental destruction in the past — and since some authors still want to measure out all ecological policies according to purely human wants and needs — we have no choice but to dispense with all notions of human distinctiveness and instead emphasize that humans, like all creatures, are just one piece in a larger cosmic puzzle. [6]

But to embrace these new teachings, one is forced to dispense with the clear biblical teaching that humanity is distinct because of God's having endowed us — and no other creatures — with his own image. We are not merely the "ashes of dead stars" who have somehow gained the ability to think and act. Rather, we are graced with the ability to think and act because God made us to be his special representatives on this planet. We are lords over this world not simply because we are smarter than most animals or more mobile than most plants but purely because God reveals this to be our status.

But if McFague and others are wrong to claim that we are not God's designated rulers of this world and yet Krauthammer and Sirico are also wrong in saying that as human beings we have the right to lord our wants, needs, and desires over all other creatures, then where does the truth lie?

The Divine Mirror

Then God said, "Let us make man in our image, in our likeness, and let them rule over the fish of the sea and the birds of the air, over the livestock, over all the earth, and over all the creatures that move along the ground." So God created man in his own image, in the image of God he created him; male and female he created them. God blessed them and said to them, "Be fruitful and increase in number; fill the earth and subdue it. Rule over the fish of the sea and the birds of the air and over every living creature that moves on the ground."

Genesis 1:26–28

In determining humanity's relationship to the creation we must begin with the biblical teaching that God created human beings in his own image. Despite the fact that there are only a handful of Bible verses that talk about the image of God

— and despite the fact that even these passages do not spell out what it means to bear God's likeness — this teaching nevertheless has become an enormously important doctrine in Christian theology. But if the Bible's treatment of the image of God is so modest, why has this idea become so important? Furthermore, if even the Bible does not specifically define the image of God for us, how do we know just what the image of God is?

First, scholars regard this doctrine to be so important because we first find it in the creation account. It is highly significant that at the first place human beings are mentioned in the Bible they are immediately described as having been made in the image of God. Clearly this image is central to understanding humanity's first, best nature.

Christian theologians have long asserted that the Bible's presentation of the creation is our best clue as to what God's intentions for this world are. Thus, we take seriously this divine designation of image bearers. In other words, the original creation is our reference point for determining what we and this entire world are supposed to be like. In this way Genesis 1–2 is like a dictionary: If we are not sure what this world or our lives in it are supposed to be like, we can refer to the original creation to give us all of the proper "spellings" and correct definitions. The creation account is God's cosmic blueprint. The more familiar we are with the original divine design, the better equipped we will be to spot where the world has gone wrong now that sin has spoiled God's plans.

So whatever we find in the Bible's presentation of creation should govern how we approach and assess life. Since this same creation account is where we find words about humanity's being made in God's image, we accept that this identity should be our first, truest definition of what a human person is. We were made to be somehow reminiscent of our divine Creator. Each of us is a mirror in which others should be able to behold God's likeness.

If sin had not come into our world, we would bear this image naturally, without even having to think about it. But because sin has corrupted us, bearing God's image has become a vocation, a task we need to work hard on lest layers and layers of sin lard over the image, obscuring godlikeness from sight. In short, we now need to be delivered of our sin if we are going to come even close to looking like God.

Not surprisingly, therefore, the Bible talks about the image of God also in the New Testament in connection to Jesus Christ. Jesus is called the perfectly expressed image of God, "the exact representation of [God's] being" (Heb. 1:3). Jesus "is the image of the invisible God" (Col. 1:15), who is filled with glory because he "is the image of God" (2 Cor. 4:4). Since Jesus was free from the stain of sin, he was the first human being since Adam and Eve who bore God's image perfectly.

Thus, New Testament writers like the apostle Paul tell us that as we become more like Jesus, the image of God that was so damaged by sin is repaired and renewed in us. The more we look like Jesus, the more we look like God. The more we look like God, the more we return to who we were created to be in the beginning. After all, as baptized believers we have "put on the new self, which is being renewed in knowledge in the image of its Creator" (Col. 3:10).

Since we find talk of the image of God in connection to both the original creation and to our redemption in Christ, theologians have properly concluded that despite the Bible's relatively modest treatment of the divine image, it is nevertheless a vital key to unlocking the mystery of human identity. In the beginning we were made to look like God. In Christ we are re-created to look like God once again. Obviously, being image bearers is central to our humanity.

But what does it mean to bear this image? What can we do to be godlike? A full answer to these questions would require a book all its own. After all, if the renewal of God's image in us through Jesus means imitating Jesus' way of life, then we know that bearing God's image is rich, not simple, involving the full range of Christian living. Bearing the divine image includes bearing the fruit of the Spirit, living within the boundaries of God's biblical laws, and just generally being holy as Jesus is holy.

For our purposes here, however, it will suffice to see that already in Genesis 1 we are given a partial clue as to what it means to be an image bearer. For no sooner than the author of Genesis mentions humanity's being made in God's image does he immediately mention two other things: the fact that we were made male and female and the fact that we have been given the charge to rule over this world and all its creatures. Although Genesis 1 does not obviously define the image of God for us, many theologians have properly concluded that these two items lend content to the image of God. Somehow our being male and female and our being put in charge of the planet tie in with our looking like God.

Some theologians, including Karl Barth, have speculated that the male-female portion of the divine image has at least two emphases: first, being male and female allows us to procreate. God creates on a grand scale, but the people made in God's image are enabled to re-create life on a smaller scale. God made Adam and Eve in his image, but now Adam and Eve have the godlike ability to make still more images of God by their having babies.

Additionally, Barth and others have asserted that the male-female part of the divine image points to the essential relatedness of human beings. We were made to forge relationships and to live in communities. Just as God exists in a holy community of three persons — Father, Son, and Holy Spirit — so also we are made in God's image to exist in relationships of union and love. The closer we are as spouses, friends, congregations, and families, the more we resemble the three Persons of the Trinity — three persons who are so close that they truly do constitute just one God.

But for our purposes we need to focus on the second item that Genesis 1 mentions in connection with image-bearing: our ruling over the earth. Apparently our having been made in God's image enables us to rule over the earth even as it obligates us to do this ruling in a way that is consistent with God's own style. We are God's vice-regents, placed on this earth to take care of it for God in a way that bears striking resemblance to how God himself would take care of it. In other words, if we do not look like God in how we treat this universe and all the creatures in it, then we are not being true to God's original design for us but are instead once again allowing sin to smear God's image to the point that it is all but lost from sight.

The Lord Keep You

> The LORD God took the man and put him in the Garden of Eden to work it and take care of it.
>
> Genesis 2:15

Genesis not only tells us we are rulers over the earth but also forces us to grapple with this basic question: What does it mean to be a godlike ruler over the fish of the sea, the birds of the air, and the creatures that move on the ground?

In Genesis 2:15 God's image bearers are given the charge to "work" and "take care of" the creation — or as other translations render the verse, we are to "tend and keep" the creation. As Calvin DeWitt has discovered, however, the same verb translated as "work" or "tend" is in other places translated as "serve."[7] We may be placed in a position above the other creatures of this world, but that position clearly obligates us first of all to service.

The other word in Genesis 2:15 is even more significant. For the word translated as "take care of" or "keep" is the same one used in the great Aaronic benediction from Numbers 6:24: "The LORD bless you and keep you." When a minister in church closes a worship service with this benediction, why are we glad to hear that God is going to "keep" us?

Is it not because we know that such divine keeping implies a protective nurturing, a providential attending to our health and safety? Indeed, this same Hebrew verb *(shamar)* is used also in the stirring conclusion to Psalm 121: "The LORD will keep [*shamar*] you from all harm — he will watch over [*shamar*] your life; the LORD will watch over [*shamar*] your coming and going both now and forevermore." If God's keeping of us means his careful, attentive, providential guarding of all that we are and all that we have, then our keeping of God's world should mean the same — we will guard, preserve, attend to, and protect all that is God's.

Yet we have not always understood Genesis in this way. Indeed, since the 1960s almost every Christian book and article written on the subject of the environment has tried to defend Genesis 1 against a now-famous charge made by historian Lynn White Jr. In a 1967 article titled "The Historical Roots of our Ecologic Crisis," White claimed that the Judeo-Christian tradition — with its biblical insistence that human beings dominate, rule, and subdue the earth — must bear the lion's share of the blame for most of our world's current pollution and degradation.

According to White, Christianity is a solidly anthropocentric or human-oriented religion. "Christianity, in absolute contrast to ancient paganism and Asia's religions, not only established a dualism of man and nature, but also insisted that it is God's will that man exploit nature for his proper ends. Hence we shall continue to have a worsening ecologic crisis until we reject the Christian axiom that nature has no reason for existence save to serve man."[8]

In other words, according to White, Christians believe God handed humanity this world on a platter to do with as we see fit. The result has been a despotic reign of terror. Since, according to Genesis, human beings are the crown of creation, we have felt free to plunder this earth for our benefit, regardless of what the larger effects have been on the other creatures with whom we share the planet.

Of course, as many writers have pointed out, some of this world's worst pollution and degradation have occurred not only in Western societies where the Judeo-Christian ethos has had the strongest influence but also in the Far East where religions like Hinduism and Buddhism are far more dominant (this despite White's claim that the religions of Asia are more eco-friendly than Christianity). Also, some of the worst pollution of this century has taken place in communist nations like the former Soviet Union and East Germany, places where the government officially eschewed all religion, starting with Christianity.

Still, as we saw from Robert Sirico, we cannot deny that some Christians, past and present, have interpreted God's words about ruling and subduing in just the ways people like White claim. But this is a radical departure from the spirit of Genesis 1 as well as from the witness of the larger Bible. For whatever Genesis's words about ruling and subduing may mean, they cannot trump the significance of God's demand that we "keep" this world with just as much thoughtful care as we hope God himself will exercise in "keeping" us.

Recently, however, author E. Calvin Beisner has claimed we should not try to understand Genesis 1's words about "ruling and subduing" in the light of Genesis 2's "serve and keep" mandate in that the two passages are not, strictly speaking, talking about the same thing. According to Beisner, in Genesis 1 God's image bearers are charged to rule and subdue the earth — presumably the entire earth. In Genesis 2, however, the more tender "serve and keep" command is applied only to the Garden of Eden. On this reading of the Genesis text the Garden of Eden was a perfectly crafted place for Adam and Eve that required no more than tender loving care and minor maintenance. The rest of the earth outside of Eden, however, was not so lovely or perfect and so required a firmer, harsher hand to beat it back and make it mind. Thus, Beisner concludes: "[I]t would have made little sense to tell Adam to subdue and rule the Garden. It was already in perfect order. But the rest of the earth apparently lacked some of the fullness of the perfection of the Garden. It was Adam's task to transform all of the earth (to subdue and rule it) into a Garden while guarding the original Garden lest it lose some of its perfection and become like the unsubdued earth. [This] implies that much that we find in the earth would not, without human transformation, have been as God intends it to be *even had the Fall and the Curse never occurred*" (emphasis in original). [9]

Beisner's perspective, however, does violence to the biblical text and calls into question the integrity of God's creative work as Genesis 1 so elegantly presents it to us. First, Beisner fails to recognize that Genesis 2 is not, as he puts it, merely a "repetition" of Genesis 1 but is a different theological presentation of the creation altogether. Nothing in Genesis 2 contradicts the beautiful truths of Genesis 1 — indeed, Genesis 2 broadens and deepens our understanding of God's creation and so ultimately builds on Genesis 1. Still, it is clearly a different account.

For instance, in Genesis 1 God creates this world's rich variety of plant life on the third day of creation. Human beings are not created until the sixth day. In

Genesis 2, however, we are told that God made Adam before any shrub or plant had been created. Additionally, Genesis 1 presents the creation of the man and the woman as a simultaneous event on that final sixth day of creation. In Genesis 2, however, Adam is alone without a female counterpart for some time. Eve is finally created sometime later after all of the other creatures were made by God and after they were all named by Adam.

Genesis 2 is not, therefore, merely a repetition or a mirror image of Genesis 1. Instead, it elaborates and expands our understanding of the divine revelation begun in the Bible's opening chapter. As such, we need to recognize that in Genesis 2, the Garden of Eden is not separate from the rest of the earth prior to the fall into sin but is instead to be seen as representing the entire earth (the part stands for the whole). Thus, God's words to "tend and keep" the Garden can properly nuance and qualify our understanding of the "rule and subdue" words in Genesis 1. The Garden of Genesis 2 stands for the entire creation.

But there is yet another reason to reject the idea that we can distinguish between the well-ordered Garden of Genesis 2 and the less-than-complete earth of Genesis 1: to do so undermines the perfection of the entire creation as Genesis 1 presents it. Among the richest theological and pastoral truths of the Bible's opening chapter is the idea that God triumphed over chaos by fashioning the creation into a well-ordered cosmos.

There is not a hint or a whisper in Genesis 1 that when the seventh day of rest rolled around, the created earth was somehow still less than God had intended. Indeed, given Genesis 1's lovely presentation of God's detailed and attentive labor over his creation of the earth, it borders on heresy to suggest that beyond the boundaries of Eden, Adam and Eve had to beat back and subdue a recalcitrant and imperfect creation lest it threaten the *shalom* of the Garden.

In short, "the earth" of Genesis 1 and "the Garden" of Genesis 2 can appropriately be seen as referring generally to the entire creation of God. Hence it is also legitimate and biblically correct to allow the tender images of Genesis 2 to qualify and enhance our understanding of the "rule and subdue" words we find in Genesis 2.

Beyond these textual features in Genesis, however, there are still more reasons to recognize that our human rule of the earth must be tender and attentive. After all, Genesis's words on this subject come in the larger context of what it means to bear God's image. Thus, it is no surprise that our keeping of the earth is to be a clear, mirrorlike reflection of God. We are to serve and preserve, to love and tenderly hold the creation, ruling it not in a despotic way but in a godlike way. For like Jesus, we are most like God when we rule by becoming a servant.

A Lord Like Jesus

It was I who taught Ephraim to walk, taking them by the arms.... I led them with cords of human kindness, with ties of love; I lifted the yoke from their neck and bent down to feed them.

Hosea 11:3a, 4

Your attitude should be the same as that of Christ Jesus: Who ... made himself nothing, taking the very nature of a servant.... Therefore God exalted him to the highest place ... [that] every tongue [might] confess that Jesus Christ is Lord.

Philippians 2:5, 7a, 9a, 11a.

One of the basic principles of hermeneutics — of biblical interpretation — is that Scripture interprets Scripture. Believing that the entire Bible was inspired by the same Holy Spirit, and believing therefore that in its teachings the Bible does not contradict itself, Christians have long asserted that one of the first places to go in interpreting a difficult Bible passage is to other, clearer Bible passages that may shed some light on or provide some clues as to what the knotty passage means.

In other words, sometimes the key to unlocking the mysteries of one part of the Bible can be located in a different part of that same Bible. Indeed, we used this principle when we looked to other passages to determine what Genesis means when it commands us to "keep" the earth. What the word *keep* means in Numbers 6 and Psalm 121 clues us in to what it means in Genesis 2.

Similarly for the larger question of what it means for human beings to "rule" the earth: If this ruling is part of God's image in us, we must rule the way God rules. So what does the rest of the Bible tell us about the nature of such godly rulership? C. S. Lewis once wrote that in this matter — as in all matters — there is a right way and a wrong way to rule. We can either rule in a godlike, lawful way or we can do it in a sacrilegious, demonic way. The better of these two ways can be seen throughout the rest of the Bible, but preeminently in Jesus Christ.

So what might ruling and dominion look like if it is to be done in such a way that others might say, "Why, that's just how God would do it"? We can begin answering that question by thinking about the doctrine of providence. After all, providence tells us how God rules and takes care of this world and our lives in it. So what is providence like? In a lovely phrase, the Heidelberg Catechism describes God's providence as that "almighty power by which he upholds, as with his hand, heaven and earth and all creatures." Indeed, we are told that all things come from "his fatherly hand."

Though described as an almighty power, there is no denying the gentle tenderness of this image. God is not a despot who ruthlessly rules everything with a heavy hand. Rather, God rules gently with a fatherly hand — the same parentlike gentleness that emerges from that beautiful passage in Hosea 11. There God depicts himself as being the proud parent who takes his children by the hand as they slowly learn how to walk.

Although God surely is sovereign and supreme, the images that cluster around his supremacy are tender and gentle. The nature of God's dominion over all things is akin to how a good parent rules over a household — in ways that are loving and kind. Such is the nature of God's dominion. We could also recall the tender images Jesus proffered when reminding his disciples that it is God who robes the fields in flowers of splendor. Likewise it is God who has his eye upon the sparrow, seeing to its needs and bringing it the food it needs to thrive. Apparently God's superintending of this world is attentive and tender.

A second place we could look in determining the nature of godlike rulership is the lordship of Christ. The claim "Jesus is Lord" is among the earliest and most scandalous of all Christian confessions. As Matthew Fox has pointed out, if we want to proclaim Christ as Lord, then that means he is Lord of all. As the apostle Paul also writes in Colossians 1, Christ is the firstborn of all creation, including not just human beings but all creatures.

Although there may be important qualitative differences between Christ's redeeming a human soul and his redeeming the earth, the fact is that Christ has redeemed all of it — body and soul, earth and heaven, human beings and the creatures of this world. Jesus is Lord over all creation. He is the one through whom it was created, and he is the one through whom it has all been reclaimed.

But in what manner did Jesus achieve his cosmic lordship? Through the humble, self-emptying, servantlike life and death that is so memorably depicted in Philippians 2. Christ did not achieve lordship through force or by wielding power with a heavy hand but instead by letting his power slip through the holes in his pierced hands. Further, now that he is Lord, he continues to exercise his lordly power through humility, through being the servant of the whole church and of the entire creation. The single most memorable biblical depiction of

Jesus' overall attitude toward his lordship is in John 13, when Jesus takes a towel and basin and washes his disciples' feet. Although the disciples were bewildered by this act — and although Peter loudly protested his Master's doing one of the dirtiest of all human services — Jesus made clear that this is what it means to be "in charge" in his kingdom. You rule by serving.

Jesus is Lord, and one day every knee will bow and every tongue will confess him as such. But the style of Christ, the way of his becoming and being Lord, is through servanthood, through self-emptying, through his deferring to others. Such is the nature of Christ's lordship over all creation.

The conjunction of God's larger providence and of Christ's lordship helps us to understand more fully our role as rulers of creation made in the image of God. Does ruling the earth on God's behalf entail power and heavy-handedness? Does God's command for us to "subdue the earth" give us a blank check to do with it what we will, to measure our deeds only against the standard of humankind and its needs?

If the doctrine of providence and the lordship of Christ have any bearing on our thinking, we must certainly say that any hint of violent, wanton, or anthropocentric domination is ruled out of order. Such attitudes represent a clear break from the divine style. For human beings to do with this world as they wish, for men and women to live in this world in such a way as to disregard other creatures, would be a profoundly ungodly thing to do.

Subduing the earth, being its lords, and dominating nature involve service to the other creatures of this world, keeping them even as we pray God will keep us. Our stance toward the creation must be Christlike through our deferring to other creatures, serving them with the cruciform, pierced hands of Christ.

Perhaps part of what such service involves is helping God's creatures live the uniqueness with which God endowed them. Christ's servant lordship led him to die for us so we could once again be all God created us to be in the beginning. Jesus restores our created humanity. So also our serving God's world means we ought to give each creature its due by letting it be what God made it to be.

Sallie McFague recently criticized what could be called the "Disney-azation" of the animal world. Cartoons frequently caricature animals, making them seem less like real lions, mice, or baboons and more like cute little human beings. The desire to be connected to and to have relationships with the animal world is good, but we should relate to animals as they are, not as we would wish them to be. [10]

Similarly, in the novel *Black Beauty* one sees horses suffering when their cruel riders cinch up the horse's necks so the horses can "look proud" as they strut around parade grounds. Unhappily, this posture is so unnatural for horses that much of their natural strength is sapped; they can no longer assume a normal posture by which to get their powerful backs into their work.

As image bearers of the Creator, we should give God's original designs for each creature room to flourish. As Richard Mouw writes, "[T]o enjoy the non-human creatures doesn't mean making believe that they are human beings. Nor does it mean treating them as mere objects to be manipulated by us for our own profit or pleasure. It means allowing them to be the 'kinds' that God created them to be." [11]

By way of example Mouw points to a gathering of Christian farmers at which the farmers lamented farming practices that tended to see chickens as no more than feathery bundles of dark and white meat. It is this shallow view of chickens that permits some factory farmers to cram chickens into row upon row of small cages in dark, warehouselike barns. In contrast, these Christian farmers concluded that "chickens should be given an open space in which to parade in front of other adult chickens, and to chase their young, and even to go off to their own private little corners to brood for a while." As Mouw comments, "These farmers weren't romanticizing chickens ... but as one of them said, 'Chickens are chickens, after all, and they deserve to be *treated* like chickens!'" [12]

If we are to remind others of our great God in whose image we were fashioned and after whose image we are renewed in Christ, then we need to exercise precisely the tender, motherly-fatherly compassion of God that these Christian men and women were seeking to incarnate into their own vocation as farmers. Only in this way can we show the loving face of the Creator to every creature under our care.

Preserving Creation's Chorus

The Ecology of Praise 3

The Peaceable Kingdom

In his collection of writings, *The Longing for Home,* Frederick Buechner recounts a visit to Sea World in Orlando, Florida. On a glorious afternoon, Buechner, his wife, and their daughter sat in the packed bleachers to watch a killer whale show. The show was run by several handsome young men and beautiful young women in bathing suits and featured the twists, turns, leaps, and splashes of five or six magnificent whales.

Buechner writes: "What with the dazzle of sky and sun, the beautiful young people on the platform, the soft southern air, and the crowds all around us watching the performance with a delight matched only by what seemed the delight of the whales, it was as if the whole creation — men and women and beasts and sun and water and earth and sky and, for all I know, God himself — was caught up in one great, jubilant dance of unimaginable beauty. And then, right in the midst of it, I was astonished to find that my eyes were filled with tears." [1]

Buechner says that afterward his wife and daughter also admitted to having shed tears during the show. A couple of years later Buechner told this story at a preachers convention in Washington only to have a British priest come up to him after the lecture to say that he had recently been at Sea World and that he too had discovered tears in his eyes while watching the spectacle.

Buechner concludes, "I believe there is no mystery about why we shed tears. We shed tears because we had caught a glimpse of the Peaceable Kingdom, and it had almost broken our hearts. For a few moments we had seen Eden and been part of the great dance that goes on at the heart of creation. We shed tears because we were given a glimpse of the way life was created to be and is not." [2]

Perhaps you also have had such an experience at one time or another. Somewhere, somehow for a shimmering moment you saw how glorious things should be only to have something startle you back to the reality of a fallen world.

At Acadia National Park in Maine a popular tourist stop is a place called Thunder Hole. Over time the incessant crashing of the waves has created a deep crevice in a rocky cliff along the shore of the Atlantic Ocean. Now as the waves sweep into this crevice, they force out the air in a thunderous "Whoosh!" It is a fun place to witness the ocean's power, even receiving a refreshing, salty spray from the sea.

Yet so often when the waves subside for a moment and the foam dissipates, visitors spy cigarette butts and gum wrappers bobbing in the water at the mouth of the crevice. Suddenly, what should have been a time of unalloyed delight is sullied by other people's mindlessness. Such an unhappy experience is reminiscent of a famous antipollution television advertisement from the early 1970s. In the ad a Native American is standing by a highway just as a load of trash is tossed out of a passing car. As the garbage explodes at the Indian's feet, he turns to the camera, two big tears rolling down his cheeks. So it is for anyone who loves God's world.

Additionally, if you watch television nature shows, you know that almost every one of these National Geographic–type specials ends the same way. Most such shows spend the first forty-five minutes showing lovely footage of coral reefs, rain forests, or wetlands, detailing the beauty and intrigue of damselfish on a reef, parrots in Brazil, caribou in Alaska, penguins at the South Pole. But then, before the show is finished, fifteen minutes or so are devoted to all of the ways by which this ecosystem is being sullied, spoiled, eaten away, or destroyed by pollution, by the encroachment of human civilization, by over-hunting and poaching, or by some other such indicator of decay.

Suddenly you, the viewer, discover your joy transforming into a minidepression. It was all so beautiful, so uplifting, so inspiring. Yet you end the viewing experience feeling discouraged. You become distressed that behind every silver lining in creation there is a cloud. And, like Buechner and the Native American in the TV ad, perhaps you find your eyes filling up with tears for how out of sync things are compared with how they are supposed to be.

Living Life's Design

How should we respond to such godly sorrow? When as Christians we sense that life and this world are at odds with what God intends, what do we typically do? Ordinarily we fight the sin, the evil, the decay, and the disarray that is working against God's designs for life in this world. In a way, the whole of the Christian life is one grand, extended attempt to behave, think, and exist in ways that line up both with how we were created in the beginning and with how we will be re-created in the kingdom of God. In short, we live in ways that bring God joy.

The Bible presents our blueprint for just this kind of godly, grateful living. So we follow the Bible to help us to color inside the lines God has drawn, to live happily within the boundary fences God has built. If we find ourselves or others coloring outside God's lines or attempting to widen the boundaries of life by moving God's moral fences to more convenient locations, then we repent and try to return to living gladly within the original design.

We recognize these dimensions to the Christian life quite easily in most areas. For instance, most Christians readily admit that sin has corrupted human sexuality, resulting in sexual desires and practices that run counter to God's design. So when we see teenagers experimenting with sex, when we pass by a rack of pornographic magazines, when we see marriages crumbling because of the wound of an adulterous affair, or when we witness a young girl who has been psychologically maimed because of some adult's sexual molestation of her, we recoil. We grieve. We shed tears at how far we have fallen from the sexual joy God intended when he created us male and female.

Of course, honesty causes us to admit that even short of these extreme sexual problems, each of us struggles with temptations in this area. Jesus said that every time we mentally undress someone or fantasize about being in some compromising position with that attractive woman or that handsome man, then we are guilty of committing "adultery in our hearts." When we read those stern words, few if any of us could ever honestly deny we also are guilty of this type of mental adultery.

Again, this causes us grief. So how do we respond? If we are Christians, we repent of these sins and temptations — repent of them but then also move forward with a still greater determination to live as God would have us to live. We may never achieve sexual purity in this life, but because the Bible shows us what God's ideal is, we do our spiritual level best to live up to that ideal. After all, you cannot imagine a devout Christian ever saying, "You know, some day God is going to re-create me into the kind of sexual being I was meant to be. So for now I'm going to couple with whomever and whatever I can and not worry about it! God will fix things later anyway, so let the orgy begin!"

Of course no sane Christian would say or think such a thing! For Christians believe that God has established a moral order. We believe we have been re-created in Christ so we can begin now to live joyfully and happily into those holy patterns. So we strive to be sexually pure, to bear the fruit of the Spirit, to live as Jesus lived all because we have been shown what kingdom living looks like. We know that this is the best way to live, we know that living this way shows our love for God, and so we want to live this way now.

But why does it so often seem that we do not adopt the same mindset toward the creation? In this area, as surely as in an area like sexuality, the Bible shows us what God's intentions and desires are. But if sin threatens and diminishes the goodness of creation, if sin corrupts the larger creation just as surely as it corrupts sexuality, and if this corruption of creation causes God sorrow just as surely as does sexual corruption, then are we not just as obligated to preserve the creation as we are to preserve our God-given moral integrity?

Yet some Christians seem to think that since God will one day restore this whole creation anyway, we need not worry about its decay now. It is going to get worse before it gets better, and since only God can make it better in the end, we will focus on other, more spiritual matters for now and simply allow the creation to slide into its inevitable, end-time decay.

But if it is wrong to take this kind of a nonchalant, devil-may-care attitude toward the disintegration of the Christian moral life, then it is just as wrong to take this attitude toward the disintegration of God's larger creation. Of course, not everyone would agree that restoring the physical creation has the same priority in the Bible as restoring the moral order of human beings. Some would claim that the general thrust of the Bible, and particularly of the New Testament, is in the direction of saving people from their sins and not saving the earth from ecological evils. As Robert Whelan succinctly puts it in *The Cross and the Rain Forest*, "It is part of God's plan for us [that] we work out our salvation in this world in preparation for eternity with him in the next. The idea that in so doing we could possibly be ... infringing the territory of other species is not one which the Christian mind can easily entertain. Jesus Christ did not die on the cross for Gaia or for the wetlands or for the rain forests, but for us."[3]

But is that so? Of course, inasmuch as the Bible is a book to be read by human beings and not grizzly bears, it makes sense that a great deal of the Bible will address human concerns and problems. But is it the case that the Bible has little or no interest in the restoration of the physical cosmos and its welter of creatures? Is it the case that when the Bible points us to the new kingdom of heaven that it is interested only in human beings dressed in shining white robes as they float on clouds and strum their golden harps?

Or is it the case that even biblical prophecies of the world to come are far more all-encompassing than this narrow, humanity-only focus? We will now examine a couple of prophecies that point us to what we usually refer to as "heaven" to see just how broad, cosmic, and downright earthy the Bible's vision of that kingdom really is. Indeed, some Christian theologians have recently begun to write about "the greening of eschatology," for we are at long last retrieving the Bible's down-to-earth vision of the world to come.

The Verdant Wilderness

> The desert and the parched land will be glad; the wilderness will rejoice and blossom. Like the crocus, it will burst into bloom; it will rejoice greatly and shout for joy.
>
> Isaiah 35:1–2

> "Instead of the thornbush will grow the pine tree, and instead of briers the myrtle will grow. This will be for the LORD's renown, for an everlasting sign, which will not be destroyed."
>
> Isaiah 55:13

> "Behold, I will create new heavens and a new earth. The former things will not be remembered, nor will they come to mind.... The wolf and the lamb will feed together, and the lion will eat straw like the ox, but dust will be the serpent's food. They will neither harm nor destroy on all my holy mountain," says the LORD.
>
> Isaiah 65:17, 25

Isaiah, like other Old Testament prophets, uses the image of the desert or wilderness to depict the fallenness of our world and the punishment of sin. The wilderness is that dangerous and threatening place where evil runs wild, where remnants of the precreation chaotic void can still be seen and experienced, a metaphor for all that seeks to threaten and finally unmake God's good work of creation. (Today, of course, the word *wilderness* is frequently used to describe pristine landscapes unspoiled by development or pollution. In this sense of the word the wilderness is a good, desirable thing. Additionally, we should also recognize that even this world's desert regions possess their own beauty and their own unique forms of animal and plant life — parts of the planet that are as worthy of preservation as any other. At this point, however, we are thinking about the wilderness in its primary biblical sense as that hot, dry, barren place of chaos which threatens life and flourishing; as that place that contains many pockets of the chaos God overcame in his act of creation.)

Hence, it is no surprise that in Isaiah's depiction the wilderness is a place not of delightful flowers but of sticking thorns and painful briers. The wilderness is not a verdant place of streams and pear trees but is a desolate place of dehydration and death. The wilderness is not a place in which to watch lovely creatures frolic, it is a place where scorpions sting and where vultures feast on the carcasses of the fallen. Where the devil has his way, the lush richness of the creation's exuberant life grows ever more quiet until the chorus of God's praise is muted if not finally silenced. In the wilderness no birds sing, no trees clap the hands of their branches, no rivers leap to praise God.

When depicting the state of our world, the wilderness is Isaiah's favorite image. Because of sin, Isaiah writes, our world resembles not Eden but the Sahara; not a valley of *shalom* but Death Valley. Sin brings hopelessness and despair, decay and death. Yet there is hope even in the wilderness. Indeed, in Isaiah 40:3 — a verse that has become one of Isaiah's most famous passages — Isaiah says God's Messiah will arrive smack in the midst of the wilderness. "In the desert prepare the way for the LORD; make straight in the wilderness a highway for our God." The wilderness, Isaiah predicts, will be the first place where our God will arrive, because it is the wilderness, after all, that is most in need of healing.

In the New Testament all four gospel writers pick up on and quote Isaiah 40:3 in connection with John the Baptist's announcement that in Jesus of Nazareth, God's Messiah had at long last come into our world. This Christ, the New Testament tells us, has built his holy highway in the wilderness of sin because it is precisely sin from which Jesus has come to deliver us and the whole world.

Thus it is no surprise to find Isaiah also telling us that a major part of God's cosmic salvation will be the budding, blooming, and verdant flourishing of the "desert" this world has become because of sin. As with all biblical prophecy, Isaiah's prophecy has multiple horizons of fulfillment. That is, although Isaiah wrote most immediately about the restoration of Israel to the Promised Land, we may legitimately read here also words that tell us about the ultimate restoration of the entire creation through the arrival of God's Christ.

The redemption that God has in store catches up not just human beings but also trees, shrubs, rivers, lions, lambs, and snakes. Everything in creation will be restored because everything in creation is suffering under the weight of sin as surely as are we human beings. But no one has ever given a more eloquent theological treatment of the creation's suffering than the apostle Paul, to whose New Testament prophecy we now turn.

Craning Its Neck

> The creation waits in eager expectation for the sons of God to be revealed. For the creation was subjected to frustration, not by its own choice, but by the will of the one who subjected it, in hope that the creation itself will be liberated from its bondage to decay and brought into the glorious freedom of the children of God. We know that the whole creation has been groaning as in the pains of childbirth right up to the present time.
>
> Romans 8:19–22

The apostle Paul agrees with Isaiah's grand vision of a renewed heaven and earth. Just as the biblical poets are not shy about claiming that the universe knows God and praises God, so Paul in Romans 8 gives humanlike characteristics to the nonhuman world. Paul claims there is a real sense in which the creation knows it has fallen from what it was meant to be. The creation senses that things are out of whack and it groans over the misalignment.

But Paul also says God has given the creation something more: hope. Somehow the creation knows that one day it is going to be liberated from its distress. If there is in the natural, created world a sadness over decay, there is also a sense of anticipation. The creation knows things are going to get better.

In verse 19 Paul says the creation "waits in eager expectation." The Greek word Paul employs here *(apokaradokia)* is a rare one in the Bible, but it is also a colorful one because literally it refers to a "craning of the neck." If you have ever watched a parade in which the president is to come by, or waited in an airport for the arrival of a loved one, then you know that as you wait, you tend to stand on your tiptoes and stretch your neck to look up ahead. Your eagerness results in your physically craning your neck, as though sticking your face a few inches forward will draw things to you more quickly.

This is the image Paul uses for the creation. Our world knows salvation is coming. Our world knows a moment of renewal is just around the corner, and it is so eager for it that the whole creation is craning its neck and standing on its collective tiptoes, straining to see just how close that glorious moment may be. Even though this world is groaning in the pain of pollution, extinctions, decay, and diminishment, the good news is these are pangs of birth.

Still, the process of childbirth flirts dangerously with death. These days it is quite rare to hear of a mother dying in childbirth, but not so long ago this was common. Childbirth works that border territory where the light of new life intermingles with the shadow of death. A husband watching his wife go through labor experiences a time of simultaneous joy and dread — joy at the prospect of birth but fearful dread that something could go wrong.

So it is for this world and for our observation of it: We fear death may win. We rue the winking out of species, are disheartened that pollution sullies almost every ecosystem on earth. Yet sometimes we glimpse the joy of something more. Paul declares the gospel good news that it will be this joy — and not the sadness of death — that will win the day. This creation's pains portend new life, not death. The creation will not die in this process but will successfully birth — by God's power in Christ — a new order of *shalom*. One day this world's symphony of sighs will be changed into a symphony of pure praise.

Isaiah's way of depicting this renewal is to envision a transformation of the wilderness. A wave of renewal will sweep across the earth, Isaiah says. Suddenly cool streams will spring up in the hot sand. Trees and crocuses will bloom, pine trees will replace thorns and thistles. Carnivorous lions will eat Bibb lettuce and like it so much that they will be able to curl up for naps with lambs and children.

In short, what was chaos will become cosmos again; the barren and dry place that had threatened life will become a rich placenta — a womb nourishing new life. Our human joy over this will be echoed by the joy of the entire universe. The stars will sing again, the trees will clap their hands, the mountains will leap like young goats, and all will be well in God's peaceable kingdom of *shalom*.

The Hope of Creation

The Bible is eminently realistic about the dismal state of our fallen world. But it is also eminently hopeful that God will not let it remain thus. Hope has been spread onto the soil of this earth like a good fertilizer. Its runoff seeps into every lake and river and ocean and is sucked up into every tree and cornstalk, and billows through the clouds in the sky.

As Steven Bouma-Prediger has written, we Christians need to take seriously the responsiveness of the creation. "That is to say, the common view of the natural world as essentially autonomous and unresponsive — as 'nature' — must be replaced by a perspective in which the natural world is seen as grace-full and response-able. All creation is a place of grace. And all creatures respond to the call of God to be and become, each in their own creature-specific way."[4] The creation does indeed respond to its Maker and is even now clinging to the hope God infused into this creation.

But, of course, for now we still experience also the sadness. Childbirth hurts and the pain cannot be blunted simply by the knowledge that soon a new little one will be laid onto the mother's stomach. The joy of that thought makes the pain worthwhile, but it takes away none of its wrenching, ripping, tearing hurt. Thus, for now we see the pain of our world, sense its travails, and are wounded that it must be so. This is not how things were supposed to be.

Although much of this book has celebrated the cosmic chorus of praise and the universal display of creation delights, we cannot ignore that the same wobbly-legged fawns whose births God watches with loving care are sometimes ripped to pieces and eaten alive by hungry lions. The same oceans that contain the delightful fruit of God's creative imagination sometimes swell into tidal waves that drown thousands of people in places like Bangladesh. As a friend of mine once said, sometimes nature seems to be speaking out of both sides of its mouth: one moment singing a song of praise to God, the next spewing out vicious roars of terror and destruction.

Of course, it is possible to see the grandeur of the power of God's creation in waves and hurricanes, but as with so much else in this world, we cannot really enjoy these awesome displays of power because they routinely threaten the life and flourishing of both the human and the nonhuman creation. Whether such fierce displays of the creation's raw energy will be on display in the new creation, we may not know for certain. But that such phenomena will no longer "harm or destroy" on God's holy mountain is certain.

For now, however, the pain of the creation remains distressingly evident. Indeed, a great many people are waking up to the distress of this world. The question for many has become, How do we respond to this pain? These days a great many believe the solution to the environmental crisis lies in deifying Mother Earth. The earth, not God, becomes the source of our life. Even some Christian theologians now revel in the image of the earth as our mother, as the one who gave us our life and who suckles us at her divine "breasts." Such images appear useful to some in that, of course, few people would ever wish to abuse their moms, so why would we ever abuse Mother Earth?

Others who are more directly outside of the Judeo-Christian ethos take all of this a step further by calling the earth a goddess, worshiping and venerating the earth accordingly. The good news of these developments is that some of these New Age approaches do result in people's being better caretakers of this world. The bad news is that elements of these false teachings are seeping into the Christian church, detracting not only from orthodoxy but also from a right apprehension of our hope.

Though it is vital that we maintain a firm distinction between the Creator and the creation, we must not be guilty of making God and creation so distinct that we evacuate spirituality from physical concerns such as the survival of the bald eagle or the flourishing of coral reefs. Lynn White Jr., who lays much of the blame for the current state of this world at the feet of the Western Christian tradition, alleges, among other things, that Christianity sanctions the rape of the earth because the Christian God is so transcendent and hence is so far removed from the physical universe that Christians do not even associate God with the earth. Whereas animistic religions locate the gods in things like trees and rivers, Christianity evacuates God from the universe by insisting that God is the wholly other — a purely spiritual being who dwells in light inaccessible in remote regions of "heaven."

Of course, White is partly right. We do not believe that God and any part of the universe are identical. That does not mean, however, that we believe God and the universe are neatly separable, as though God is wholly unconcerned with what happens to the physical world he made. Although this separation is not a biblical teaching, it seems many Christians have made and continue to make just this conclusion.

Certainly this can be seen in some of the more ascetic extremes in Christian history. There have been those who have believed that the only way properly to focus on God is to eschew as much of the physical life of the body as possible. So celibacy replaced an active sexuality, meager diets of bread and water replaced more sensuous meals, simple and drab garments replaced flashier fabrics, prayer and Scripture reading replaced a more active life in the world of commerce or agriculture.

But is such an austere, antiphysical life necessary to apprehend or worship our God? The Bible would seem to indicate that it is not. Indeed, one of the earliest heresies of the Christian church was Gnosticism, one of whose central doctrines was a Greeklike disdain for the physical and the bodily in favor of a focus on only the spiritual and ethereal.

Although long ago condemned as a heresy, elements of Gnosticism can still be found in the wider church. How often do we not still teach our children to picture heaven as a place as completely unlike this physical earth as possible? How often do we picture heaven not as Isaiah's paradise of soaring mountains, bubbling brooks, and delicious pears but as a wispy, vapory place of golden streets in which we will flit and float around like Caspar the Friendly Ghost? (Of course, the Bible also uses some of these wispier images, but they are not the only images in the Bible nor are they the primary ones used to depict the new creation.)

How readily we forget the second-to-the-last line of the Apostles' Creed: "I believe in the resurrection of the body." We will have real bodies of renewed flesh and blood in heaven. We will be able to eat and drink just as surely as Jesus ate and drank with his disciples following his own resurrection from the dead.

Christianity is, after all, an incarnational religion. That is, we believe that our God took on flesh and blood to save us body and soul and that once salvation was accomplished, we are further promised a renewed body with which we will one day enjoy a renewed earth. Christianity is finally an earthly religion. We look forward to the renewal of mountains, lakes, streams, fingernails, hair, and lungs and not to their decimation.

It is for this reason that, as C. S. Lewis once said, we Christians need always to be fighting on two fronts. On the one front are the pantheists who think that everything is divine. When you are dealing with them, you need to emphasize that God and creation are distinct. On the other front are those who make the chasm between God and creation so deep and wide that in their service to God they care not a fig for the environment. When dealing with these folks, Lewis says, you need to emphasize how close God is to his creation, pointing out that in a sense God really is in my dog, my cabbage patch, my oak tree. It is a delicate balancing act between identifying God too closely with the world and not keeping God close enough. [5]

Ultimately, the main difficulty with the views presented in *The Cross and the Rain Forest* is that God ends up being so far removed from the physical creation that the resulting picture borders on a form of deism. Deism teaches that although God created the universe at the dawn of time, he has since then largely been absent. Some compare this teaching to the winding up of a watch: In the beginning God gave the "watch" of this cosmos a hefty winding up, but since then he has merely allowed it to tick down on its own.

Of course, Whelan and his coauthors do not, strictly speaking, endorse deism; after all, they do believe God is invested in us human beings and in our salvation. But in the authors' presentation, God's interest in the physical world of creation seems at times limited only to human beings. People and people alone are redeemed through Jesus' death on the cross. He did not die for, and therefore does not redeem, wetlands and animals. Instead, God created the world, handed it over to humanity to use as we see fit, and since then has scarcely given his nonhuman creation a backward glance. For Whelan, Kirwan, and Haffner, God's perspective on animals never enters the picture.

Similarly, when discussing some Christian attempts to preserve trees for their beauty, Whelan claims that "even amongst Christian writers ... we find traces of an attitude toward trees which seems to regard them as more than just a source of wood." 6 But trees *are* more than just a source of wood for human beings! Trees are God's creation. The Bible pictures them as clacking their branches in praise of God even as his power and grandeur are reflected in the power and grandeur of stately oaks and the mighty cedars of Lebanon. God is highly invested in his creation of trees, and not simply because we humans can build houses with them or create a crackling bonfire out of them. (Bernhard Anderson has even noted a curious verse in Deut. 20:19 in which God tells the Israelites that when they are besieging a city, they are not wantonly to chop down the trees and forests around the city. After all, God says, the trees are not Israel's enemies.)

So why do Christians of all people so often miss this facet of creation and of the Bible? Why do some of our own teachings sometimes look less Christian and more cultlike? In the spring of 1997 the world was tantalized by the brilliant appearance of the Hale-Bopp comet — one of the first comets most people had ever seen that really looked like a comet, including a distinctly visible tail. But at least one group of people saw something more in this celestial visitor. Just a few days before Good Friday and Easter the news was abuzz with the mass suicide of the Heaven's Gate cult in California.

According to a video tape left behind by the cult's leader, the members of Heaven's Gate were convinced that this earth was destined to be "recycled" and that they had to escape this planet and hitch a ride with a UFO, which they believed was hidden within the Hale-Bopp comet. Their destiny had nothing to do with the physical life of this earth but instead lay beyond in some wispy spiritual dimension accessible only by an alien spacecraft.

This cult's teaching is clearly an heir of the ancient heresy of Gnosticism and its shunning of all things earthly. (Further evidence of their asceticism is the fact that the males in this cult had all been castrated). Occasionally, however, elements of this disdain can be detected within the Christian church. Although author Hal Lindsey never claimed that the earth was soon to be "recycled," the title of his best-selling book in the 1970s did sound distressingly like an obituary for all things earthly: *The Late, Great Planet Earth.* That book's title, and the dispensationalist theology within it, was also a call for Christians to prepare to "jump ship," escaping this earth in favor of the spiritual destiny of the kingdom.

It is, therefore, no surprise that at least a few fundamentalist dispensationalists are among the least ecologically concerned people in the wider Christian community. After all, Christians are called to live a kingdom life and have a kingdom vision now. But if one's picture of what "heaven" will be like contains no images of a new creation of mountains, streams, goats, and aspen trees, then the focus of life now will likewise look past these earthly splendors in favor of contemplating the vapory spiritual splendors still to come.

But this earth — and the entire cosmos — is the creation of our God. He loves it, adores it, holds it close, and has died to redeem it — to redeem all of it. Anthony Hoekema even went so far as to say that to envision the new kingdom as anything other than a renewed creation would be to concede a great victory to the devil. "If God would have to annihilate the present cosmos ... then Satan would have succeeded in so devastatingly corrupting the present cosmos and the present earth that God could do nothing with it but blot it totally out of existence." 7 But God will prove his victory over the devil by salvaging and reinvigorating the very earth that Satan has so long been working to unmake.

Thus, for Christians there is indeed a gospel hope in and for this world — a hope not found among those who think the earth is a goddess, not found among those who regard everything as divine. It is not just good orthodoxy to keep ourselves from New Age pantheism and goddess worship, it may also be the best way to live joyfully despite all of the depressing decay seen in everything from National Geographic specials to litter at Thunder Hole.

According to Francis Schaeffer, Charles Darwin, near the end of his life, wrote that as he had gotten older, two things had become dull to him: his former joy in the arts and his former joy in nature. Schaeffer noted that perhaps the atrophy of Darwin's joy in nature stemmed at least in part from his lifelong attempts to reduce this cosmos to no more than impersonal forces interacting with blind chance stretched out over an unimaginably long period of time. In this picture there is neither much hope nor joy.

Darwin's waning joy made sense to Schaeffer, but what he could not figure out was why so many orthodox Christians seemed to have a similar lack of joy in nature. We believe this world is the handiwork of a personal, purposeful God who is even now working to realize the hope he himself has given to every creature in the universe. In an ironic twist, Schaeffer noted that atheists and pantheists have no reliable guide for knowing what constitutes nature as it should be and what represents nature in a fallen state. If everything that exists is divine, then even what we would label as bad in nature is somehow also within God, not outside of him. Worse yet, atheists can only speculate on what is right and what is wrong in nature. Perhaps in the end an atheist's conclusions about what constitutes bad ecology and what constitutes good ecology would accord with our own ideas. But even so, atheists have no reliable hope that what they regard to be right and lovely in nature will eventually conquer what is wrong and destructive.[8]

But Christians know the difference between God and the universe, and we have God's own Word to tell us further how to distinguish between what is right from what is wrong in creation. But none of that is as grand as what we learn from the prophet Isaiah and from the apostle Paul: that God himself will make sure that what he intended for this creation in the beginning will in the end return and triumph. This is a hope that can further enhance our joy in creation — for we know creation will endure to be enjoyed for all eternity!

Christians look to God and his Word for guidance in all of life because we believe that only there do we find a consistent vision for this creation in the past, the present, and the future. We stick with the gospel of our Lord because we know he is the Word of God who spoke the creation into being and he will one day be the same Word of God to respeak the creation into the new order it even now cranes its neck to see.

The Bible gives us a glimpse, a vision, of what was once true of the creation and of what will be true again one day. As with Buechner at Sea World, so we sometimes catch glimpses of that peaceable kingdom. For now the disparity between what is and what is yet to come may cause us to shed tears. But it is precisely for people like us — people who love the handiwork of our God — that Jesus once said, "Blessed are you who weep now, for you will laugh."

For Whom?

But as we now live between the tears and the laughter, we recognize that as in all moral matters, so also regarding the creation: We must live in ways that accord with God's designs and wishes. We recognize we are commissioned to keep alive the welter of things that God created, that he still takes delight in, that he died to save, and that he will soon re-create.

Christians must be staunch environmentalists — or staunch creationists, to use the more biblical term — not because we have our own best interests at heart but because we have God's best interests at heart.

Recently the *Atlantic Monthly* pointed out that, left to their own devices, individuals and corporations will not do the environmentally sound thing unless it pays off financially. If it is cost effective to install antipollution devices — and it almost never is — then a factory owner will do so. Otherwise he will spew as much gunk into the river and as much sulphur into the air as he can get away with. [9]

Similarly with individuals: To my mind there are few acts as wantonly idiotic as tossing an empty pop can out a car window. Yet when I was growing up in the 1970s, our country road was regularly littered with scores of empty pop and beer cans. Only after the state made those cans worth a dime — a measly ten cents! — did people stop junking up the creation with them. Now it is rare to see such cans or bottles on the side of the road — even those that do still appear do not stay there for long, because someone usually picks them up to cash them in!

People often need to be bribed to do the right thing. But as Christians, we should not need any reasons to preserve this world other than the grand reason that God loves it. This world in all its variety praises God. But that also means that the ecology of God's praise thins down, down, down as more and more species become extinct, as rain forests are reduced to barren moonscapes, as wetlands are cemented over, as coral reefs are vandalized by jet skis.

These days environmentalists are desperately seeking spiritual reasons why we should preserve the world. Writer Alston Chase recently assembled a list of the popular religious options: Tao, Vedanta, Sufism, Cabalism, Spinozistic Pantheism, Yoga, biofeedback, transcendental meditation, Gandhian pacifism, animism, panpsychism, alchemy, ritual magic, Buddhist economics, fossil love, planetary zoning, deep ecology, shallow ecology, reinhabitation, ecological primitivism, chicken liberation, stone age economics, Yin Yang, the androgynous universe, the Gaia hypothesis, global futures, Spaceship Earth, rights of rocks, ecological resistance. [10]

Into this Babel of confusion, it is time that we Christians offer our unique and, we believe, correct perspective. What motivates a love of nature is that it is not finally "nature" at all! It is creation, it is God's work! As such it bears the stamp of his glory, it praises him in all its manifold diversity, and it has received and continues to receive his divine benediction.

Indeed, we Christians believe that the hands that are upraised to bless forests and toads are now pierced hands. For Jesus died to redeem not just hearts and souls but also this creation. When the apostle Paul writes in Romans that the whole creation is groaning in eager anticipation of its own renewal, we are vividly reminded that Jesus is the Word of God who spoke creation into being in the beginning and is the Word made flesh who died to redeem the creation once again.

As God's vice-regents over this creation, we rule this world by serving it, and we serve it in godlike, Christlike ways because we bear God's image to do just that. But what are some specific ways by which we can do all of this? The possibilities for how we can be ecologically sensitive Christians could fill up an entire book. But here are just a few basic suggestions — mere springboards for still more thinking about this subject both in our individual lives and in our corporate life together as congregations.

Let Us Preserve: Suggestions for Stewards

First, on a practical yet simple day-to-day basis within our homes, we should look at our curbside recycling bin as a holy vessel in the service of God. Although we cannot avoid leaving some trash and waste in our wake, we should do what we can to reuse everything possible lest the earth end up teeming more with our junk than with God's creatures. Likewise we turn down our heat and turn up our air-conditioning, buy more efficient toilets, turn the water off while brushing our teeth, opt for cloth diapers instead of disposables, and use carpools — all in service to the Creator.

These common, mundane activities and other ecologically sensitive actions like them may not look particularly spiritual, but if they slow down this world's decay or diminish the amount of pollutants in the air, on the land, or in the seas — if they keep alive a few more of those creatures who "day by day pour forth speech" — then we are surely pleasing God. Indeed, we are then fulfilling the earthkeeping assignment God gave us at the dawn of time. What could be more spiritual than fulfilling the very tasks and mandates God gives us in his Word?

Additionally, we would do well to remember a principle articulated by Calvin DeWitt: We should enjoy the creation's fruit without endangering its fruitfulness. [11] Biblically we must regard cows and trees, lakes and fish, as existing for more than merely human use and utility. However, this does not deny that we may use trees for making two-by-fours and sheets of paper. I do not intend to suggest that we may never eat meat, go to a fish fry, or eat a carrot. In addition to their functions as reflections of God's glory and givers of God's praise, plants and creatures are also necessary for human health, nourishment, and flourishing.

However, even this enjoyment of God's creation fruit must be done in the light of God's larger perspective on creation. It may be morally permissible to trap and eat Maine lobsters, but it is not right to over-trap those lobsters to the point that people wonder if a day may come when there will be no crustaceans left in the once lobster-rich waters of Maine. Similarly, we need trees to produce the paper this book is printed on as well as to make the beams that support the roof over our heads. Still, clear-cutting an entire forest is wrong. Or attempting to cut down a rare tree species — such as the California Redwood — is not a prudent use of the resource of God's trees but instead verges on abuse.

Whenever enjoying a certain fruit of creation means diminishing the availability of that same fruit for future generations, we fail to keep the earth lush for God, as God himself charged us to do. Whenever our actions result in a world with less variety of creatures, plants, and trees than the world we found, we grieve God as creation's chorus thins out.

As I write, I have just returned from a vacation during which I spent some time in the forests near the Sleeping Bear Dunes National Lakeshore in northern Michigan. Some of those forests are sickly and contain many dead pine trees. According to a National Parks brochure, the reason for this is that when logging companies clear-cut these forests earlier this century, they were required to replant trees in their wake. Because it is easier and quicker to go through and plant just one kind of tree seed, the logging companies did just that. However, the resulting new forest is highly susceptible to disease; if one tree gets sick, they will all quickly get sick. In a natural forest, oaks, maples, birches, pines, and aspens are all interspersed such that if one oak tree contracts a disease, it may well affect only that tree. The birches and maples near the sick oak will not be susceptible to an oak disease. Further, an oak tree a hundred yards away probably won't catch the illness either, because of its safe distance from the sick tree. But if a forest is made up only of birches, one sick tree will affect all the trees, the disease easily skipping from one tree to the next. Further, as Sallie McFague explains in her most recent book,

> Logging companies replant [old-growth forests] with a monoculture — a single species of fast-growing tree — claiming they are restoring what they have removed. Thus, they have presumably respected the right of the forest to survive. However, these monoculture forests are not only vulnerable to fire and blight, but they lack the rich, complex diverse insect, bird, and mammal life as well as the underbrush and underground root system of a natural forest with its many different kinds of trees. In fact, they are not forests at all but plantations of single-species trees. The appropriate ethic in this instance is not one of rights but of care

— paying attention to what truly constitutes forests and then providing the conditions to maintain and restore them; for instance, selective tree cutting for intact forests and reseeding for biodiverstiy in clear-cut areas. [12]

Utilizing the creation's fruit without endangering its fruitfulness requires that we respect not merely the sheer number of God's creatures in the world but also their diversity, variety, and their mutual interactions. This is a principle we can seek to uphold in our day-to-day consumption of this world's fruits.

Second, beyond what we can do in our homes, we should also support larger efforts and legislation that aim to preserve the world by curbing the sinful, demonic tendency to destroy. We should be properly alarmed when people — often fellow Christians — disdain and so seek to repeal legal efforts to preserve the earth.

Secretary of the Interior Bruce Babbit sadly notes that the past few years have witnessed precisely this disdain. As a Christian, Babbit is well acquainted with a proper interpretation of the Bible, yet he must continually battle legislators who claim that the Bible's words in Genesis allow us to do with the earth as we see fit for our maximum benefit. In recent years Babbit has witnessed legislators trying to dismantle the Clean Water Act and the Endangered Species Act. Some have lamented the outlawing of DDT, claiming that even if doing so saved the bald eagle from extinction, it nevertheless drove up the cost of doing business. Still other senators and congressional representatives have made speeches branding the Environmental Protection Agency as "the Gestapo of government." [13]

These are not uncommon complaints. Over the past few years I have presented in sermons most of the ideas found in this book. So long as my comments remained general, the members of my congregations were willing to nod their heads in approval. But whenever a sermon specifically promoted recycling or encouraged broad Christian support for earth-friendly legislation, eyebrows would go up and I would receive critical comments after the service.

Some claim current laws for clean water or for species preservation are imperfect, go too far, or simply make life miserable without really achieving anything positive in the end. Others claim agencies like the EPA are examples of our having too much government, of government worming its way into our lives. Still others say recycling is a hassle and makes such a modest dent in the amount of trash dumped every year that the entire effort is not worth the money spent on trucks, plants, and personnel.

But just because no law or government agency is perfect does not mean we would be better served without them. As Christian stewards charged by God to tend and keep the garden of this world, our "default setting" ought to be for preservation. Efforts to preserve the world should meet with Christian approval.

Consider an analogy: Most people would doubtless agree that a staunch and consistent pro-life position leads Christians to applaud and encourage any legislation that tends in the direction of fewer abortions. At most, pro-life Christians may lament that some legislation does not go far enough, but if a law is at least headed in the right direction, pro-life Christians ought to be glad.

When Bill Clinton ran for president in 1992 he claimed that he wanted to make abortions "rare." But many people have doubted the sincerity of that claim because of the kinds of laws he has supported and bills he has vetoed. When in 1996 the president vetoed the partial-birth abortion bill, he claimed it was because the bill had no allowance in it for mothers whose lives were endangered by the pregnancy. He further stated that if the bill had had such a provision, he would have signed it.

But few evangelicals bought the line of reasoning the president was selling, because, many believed, a truly pro-life person would have signed the legislation anyway as at least a small — albeit perhaps imperfect — step in the right direction. Indeed, many pro-life persons would point out that partial-birth abortions are so horrific that compromises should not even be considered by anyone who is pro-life to the core.

Similarly regarding laws and groups that work to put limits on pollution levels, development, and habitat destruction: If we are ardently pro-creation, we will support gladly any effort to keep alive God's delightful world of wonders and creation's chorus of praise. Even if such laws and groups are imperfect, even if mistakes are sometimes made, even if it could be proven that here or there a given law goes too far or does not go far enough, even if a government agency makes an unfair ruling, we are grateful even to have such safeguards in the first place. If they need fine-tuning, we should work on such refinements. But such tinkering and repair work is far better than the all-out effort to dismantle laws and agencies.

In the last twenty years many Christian leaders have been at the forefront of those pushing for less government in general, including in environmental matters. The attitude of some seems to be that businesspersons, corporations, and individuals should be free to decide for themselves on matters such as wetland preservation and emission controls. If we just leave people alone, this line of reasoning claims, they generally will do the right thing. But even if they do not, at least we have not encroached on their freedom by introducing still more government interference. (The broader notion here is known as laissez faire capitalism: People should be free to do as they see fit to increase profits, take care of their workers, and establish their own hiring policies.)

However, Christians have traditionally affirmed that left to their own devices, sinful people who are born in a depraved state will not necessarily or consistently do the right, good, God-glorifying thing. As we live between Eden and the kingdom, we are born bent away from God. It is for this reason we need civil governments. John Calvin, commenting on Romans 13 and related passages, said that the government needs to be involved in people's lives to force them to do what is agreed upon as the right and moral course of action in many areas of life. Thus in Romans 13 Paul declares that the governing officials are God's *diakonoi* or "servants" to insure order and do God's will in the civil realm.

If it is true the devil hates God's creation enough to wish it harm, then surely restraining this evil is a proper function of God's servants in government. Although government, like everything else, must have limits lest it fall into sinful extremes, it is certainly proper that we look to the law of the land to help us in our stewardly, holy task of keeping God's world clean, intact, and alive — to God's honor and glory!

Third, our church communities should be creation-friendly places. In addition to enhancing our opportunities to appreciate and delight in the creation, we should also work to insure that our churches engage in responsible stewardship practices. So we should recycle as much of our church's paper products as possible, perhaps also stop using plastic and styrofoam products at church socials in favor of utilizing the glass and ceramic plates and cups with which most church kitchens are already well stocked. We should also monitor the building's use on weekdays to insure we are not heating or cooling rooms that are never used except on Sundays.

Planning committees would do well to consider the environmental impact of building an addition or a new church edifice. They should consider purchasing lighting systems that use less energy, perhaps installing motion detectors that turn lights on when people enter a room but also shut them off when the room is not in use. (Of course, such a lighting system could be installed in existing buildings.)

But churches should also address larger questions. Will building a church on a given site damage an ecosystem or a unique habitat beyond repair? Is there a way to construct the building to minimize the number of trees that must be cut down? (A friend of mine, who runs a successful tree service, exercises his Christian identity by telling his customers he refuses to cut down healthy trees for reasons relating merely to the aesthetics of landscaping. This policy is a fine example of applying concern for creation to our everyday Christian lives and should also be part of the church's witness to the world.)

Fourth and finally, we can give money and volunteer time to organizations dedicated to preserving the environment. Whereas a few years ago such organizations were all "secular," today we can choose from a range of Christian groups.

In the past two decades a number of Christian organizations have been formed to catch the church community up with the larger effort to preserve the creation. The Evangelical Environmental Network (EEN), the Christian Environment Project, the Christian Society of the Green Cross, and the Au Sable Institute are now working to provide educational materials for churches as well as to give hands-on opportunities for Christians to help clean up soiled ecosystems. At minimum such groups are worthy of our financial support. Beyond money, we Christian stewards could also volunteer for service projects or make use of the resources now available to educate our congregations in a biblical environmental ethic.

But we need not limit ourselves only to Christian groups. Most environmental action groups do not require members to endorse non-Christian tenets — although, as is to be expected, some groups do espouse a kind of religious stew as they draw somewhat uncritically from the faith traditions represented among their many members. We need to be wary of such spiritual mixtures even as we provide a distinctive Christian witness.

However, we must also recognize and applaud groups whose overall aims line up well with Christian doctrine. The theological tenet of "common grace" teaches us that the residue of God's image remains in all people, Christian or not. Thus, non-Christian environmentalists unwittingly fulfill the "tend and keep" mandate of Genesis 1–2. (Indeed, it is an unhappy fact that some non-Christians have done a better job imitating God's tender style of earth-ruling than have some Christians.)

Organizations like the Sierra Club, World Wild Life Fund, the Audibon Society, and the Nature Conservancy as well as national park action groups like the Friends of Acadia in Maine are legitimate and vital groups to which we may contribute money and in which we may meaningfully be able to exercise godly principles of stewardship and preservation. Working in such groups provides the chance to prove to at least some in this world that when it comes to the cosmos, we Christians really are interested in more than debates about evolution. We can demonstrate we are interested in this world because we are a people highly interested in our Creator God, whom we love and to whom we want to give the glory always.

The Body

> O LORD, my God, you are very great; you are clothed with splendor and majesty.... May the glory of the LORD endure forever; may the LORD rejoice in his works.
>
> Psalm 104:1, 31

In the New Testament the apostle Paul often uses the analogy of the body to describe the church. Although the church is made up of many different people with widely varying abilities and gifts, in God's providence we need each and every one of those people and the full range of their gifts for the church to function. Paul said it would be silly for an eye to say to the foot, "I am more important than you are because I can see where we are walking." The eye may be able to see where the body is going, but take away the foot, and that body will not be going anywhere!

In a way, the same applies to this world and its variety of creatures. The Bible tells us the world is a symphony of praise to the glory of God. In an orchestra, a violinist cannot disdain a flutist; a percussionist cannot sneer at the oboe player. For to play a symphony, the orchestra needs each and every musician and instrument; without the full orchestra, the performance is diminished.

In the symphony of creation it is not up to us to determine the relative importance of one species over another. God needs and wants them all to take part; that is why he put them here in the first place! So we cannot shrug our shoulders when we hear that the dusky seaside sparrow has become extinct. We cannot pass over such a tragedy by saying, "Well, there are lots of other birds in the world." Instead we should see the creation the way God sees it: as a fundamental whole that needs all of its parts if the rich symphony of God's creation is to be played correctly and beautifully.

The time has come for Christians to keep alive every section in creation's orchestra and every voice in creation's praise chorus. As Christians, our highest devotion is to God alone. We worship God, not Mother Earth. We serve God, not ourselves. We bow the knee to God, not to any group, agency, cause, or government of this earth. But it is precisely because of what God's Word tells us about God's attitude toward his creation that we also seek ways to uphold, preserve, care for, and protect this world and its welter of creatures. For when a species of bird winks out of existence, God loses a whole section of creation's choir. When forests are clear-cut, there are fewer branches to clap their hands in praise.

Psalm 104, a gorgeous poem of creation, sings out, "May the glory of the LORD endure forever; may the LORD rejoice in his works" (v. 31). Given the nature of Psalm 104, that verse is another way of saying, "May the creation in all its rich and delightful diversity be preserved so that creation's praise chorus will continue." God has made us in his own image so we can represent him in this world. We are his chosen instruments of preservation. It is up to us to keep this part of God's visible glory alive and to let his praise continue to go forth. "The heavens declare the glory of God." Yes, they do. Let's not muffle the chorus.

THE LANDSCAPE OF
RIGHTEOUSNESS

A Meditation

First of all, you must understand that in the last days scoffers will come, scoffing and following their own evil desires. They will say, "Where is this 'coming' he promised? Ever since our fathers died, everything goes on as it has since the beginning of creation." But they deliberately forget that long ago by God's word the heavens existed and the earth was formed out of water and by water. By these waters also the world of that time was deluged and destroyed. By the same word the present heavens and earth are reserved for fire, being kept for the day of judgment and destruction of ungodly men.... But the day of the Lord will come like a thief. The heavens will disappear with a roar; the elements will be destroyed by fire, and the earth and everything in it will be laid bare. Since everything will be destroyed in this way, what kind of people ought you to be? You ought to live holy and godly lives as you look forward to the day of God and speed its coming. That day will bring about the destruction of the heavens by fire, and the elements will melt in the heat. But in keeping with [God's] promise we are looking forward to a new heaven and a new earth, the home of righteousness.

2 Peter 3:3–7, 10–13

In John Updike's latest novel, *Toward the End of Time,* we meet Ben Turnbull, a sixty-six-year-old man struggling to come to grips with his passing life and the rigors of old age. One late-November morning Ben awakens to the first snow of the season. "I awoke to see a fragile white inch on the oak branches outside the bedroom windows, and on the curving driveway below, and on the circle of lawn the driveway encloses. I looked into myself for a trace of childhood exhilaration at the sight and found none ... this radiant day [was to me] like a fresh meal brightly served in a hospital to a patient with a dwindling appetite."[1]

Too often it seems today that Christians have a similar dwindling appetite for the splendors of God's creation. The handiwork of God is on wondrous, bright, and fresh display, and yet we too often turn our faces away in distraction. We are not hungry for the splendors God is dishing up. Worse, what often lies behind our diminished appetite is the belief that genuinely spiritual matters — the gospel concerns around which we orient our lives — have little or nothing to do with ecological matters. Like Ben Turnbull, we sometimes feel we are coming toward the end of time and that the return of Christ is coming soon. In the face of that, some Christians appear to think, earthly concerns of the environment simply fade away.

The apostle Peter disagrees. Peter's second epistle is widely regarded as his last letter, and Peter himself seems to recognize that this will be so. Thus, Peter presents what is his last will and testament of the faith — the gospel inheritance he desires to bequeath to his children in the faith. Knowing it is his last chance to communicate with his fellow Christians, Peter wants to make every word count. As we conclude our reflections on God's creation of wonder and delight, it is especially interesting to note the high profile Peter gives to the creation in the closing chapter of his final letter. For in the end, Peter returns to the beginning. According to Peter, the bottom line of our gospel hope can be read in the top line of the Bible.

By the time Peter wrote this letter, members of the first generation of Christians were dying, either of natural causes or at the hands of Roman persecutors. This dying off caused a crisis because many people had believed Jesus would come again before the first generation of believers died. So as the apostolic generation waned, so did people's confidence in Jesus.

Of course, it did not help that people, both in and out of the church, had begun to scoff.

"Yeah, right! 'Jesus is coming again,' you all say. 'Jesus is Lord!' you proclaim. Well, wake up and smell the pita bread! Jesus has come and gone and nothing is different! People still get sick and die. It has been forty years since Jesus left, and yet there is not a blessed thing different about life on this old earth!"

Some in the church began to listen to these scoffers. Some began to conclude, "You know, they're right! Just look around us; we still suffer from diseases, we still hold funerals all the time, the Caesar is still the 'lord and god' of the empire and he's wiping out the apostles one by one. Soon all of them will be gone. And then what? Can we go on without the living link of the apostles? Will Jesus still be with us once his closest friends on earth are all dead?"

In answer to these fears, Peter in essence says, "Remember creation!" He tells his readers to remember what the prophets wrote and what Jesus said. Given what Peter goes on to say about the creation and the renewal of all things, it is likely that the specific prophecies he refers to here are some of the same passages we looked at in this book.

We are told to remember the great words of prophets like Isaiah, who assure us that God's peaceable kingdom will come, that a day will come when all will be made fresh and new, when the desert of this sinful world will be transformed into a new Eden, when streams will flow and fruit will grow, when the scorching places of death will become a pleasant placenta of new life. A day will come when lions and lambs will lie down together, when mountains will leap and trees will clap their hands in praise of the Creator.

These are the words Peter calls to mind. But Peter also recalls "the command of our Lord and Savior." It is difficult to know just what Peter has in mind here, though the words of the Great Commission are likely. Jesus assured his followers he would be with them "always, even to the end of the age." Jesus never said how long it would take to get to the end of the age. But he did say that no matter how long it takes, he will always be here.

Having reminded the believers of these prophecies and promises, Peter then takes on the scoffers. In refuting their claims Peter returns to the creation. In verse 5 he says the scoffers deliberately forget that once upon a time, God spoke and it was. By pointing to the power and grandeur of Genesis 1, Peter reminds his readers that if God could do that — if the very word of God could make everything from the Pleiades in the heavens to the ants on the ground — then we need not worry whether he can send Jesus back to us.

But then Peter moves from the creation to the flood to make two points. On the one hand the flood is yet another example of God's power. But on the other the flood is also evidence that God has remained involved in the world he made. God is no absentee landlord. He has remained passionately invested in what happens on this earth — so much so that when the chaos of sin seemed to be edging out the cosmos of God, God intervened to cleanse the earth with a flood. In the same way, Peter concludes, God's investment in this world will lead him to deluge it again, this time with fire.

But even though Peter predicts a destruction by fire, and even though in verse 6 he says that the world was "destroyed" by the original flood, Peter knows that as it was for Noah's flood, so it will be in the end: The result will be not destruction but renewal. Through Noah's ark God kept alive the variety of creatures he had made. When the flood waters dried up, the beautiful creation of God was still intact, ready to be reinhabited.

So in verses 10–13 Peter predicts an ultimate preservation at the end of time. Because the fire will be a renewing fire — a cleansing, not an annihilation. When the fires of God sweep over the creation, when the smoke clears and the last embers go out, what we will see will be not a scorched and barren landscape but a renewed creation. As Isaiah says, it is the power of evil that leaves behind a scorched and scorching place of destruction. But where God is, there is lush new life.

Indeed, Peter concludes in verse 13 by saying that what will result from the fire will be "the home of righteousness," or as Eugene Peterson paraphrases this passage, it will be a new creation "all landscaped with righteousness."[2] It will be a stunning thing to see.

Imagine that one night as you sleep the smoke detector goes off in the hallway and you awake to find choking smoke billowing through the house. So you rush to get everyone out safely, and then from the sidewalk you watch helplessly as flames lick out every window and fire races along the roofline.

But then imagine that just as the fire is burning brightest, suddenly it goes out. As the smoke lifts, you blink in wonder as you see before you not the burned out shell of your old house but instead a new palace. In the place of your old house with its aluminum siding and plastic shutters, there is an edifice of hewn limestone gilded with gold!

So it will be in the end, Peter says. And the good news is that because we know this is coming, we need not fear the day of the fire. We will not be terrified as galaxies and moons melt, because we know that when it is over there will be a new creation landscaped with righteousness, with the very glory of God ringing out from every singing warbler, from every leaping brook, and from every spouting whale. It will be the home of righteousness, the place where everything delightful and right will fit in naturally and well.

Such is Peter's message in some of the very last words he ever wrote. But we need to pick up on some of these themes by posing the same ultimate question Peter puts before his readers in verse 11: In the light of what's coming, what kind of people should we be?

Peter answers his own question by telling us to live holy, godly lives. That is another way of saying we are to imitate God by doing what God does. We shun what cuts against the grain of God's holiness, we love the things God loves. Included here, surely, is a life that focuses on and revels in God's creation.

Peter's diagnosis that the problem of the scoffers in his day is that they delib-erately forget creation is a curious one because it is doubtful the scoffers thought this was a problem. They would probably respond, "We're talking about this present moment and about how it does not seem to offer much promise for the future. So why are you prattling on about creation? What's the past got to do with anything?" But Peter says the problem with their view of both the present and the future is they have cut themselves off from the past. If only the scoffers would remember creation, their views on the present and future would fall into place.

In a way, that is one of the points made in this book. Too often in our view of the present and of the future, we leave out the past. If we are honest, we must admit that the doctrine of redemption looms much larger for us than does the doctrine of creation. We spend far more time thanking God for the cross than for the creation that the cross redeems; far more time pondering our identity as morally pure persons than our biblically mandated identity as image-bearing stewards of creation.

Peter would urge us to get out into God's world of wonders to praise God for what we see. He would remind us that the power of God displayed in the uni-verse is a major part of what anchors our Christian hope in God's promises. The power of God as seen in hippos and meadowlarks assures us that God both can and will keep his gospel promises to renew all things.

Peter would tell us that God's delight in his every creature should inspire our own delight and motivate us to preserve this world for God. Although Peter foresees a purging of this world by fire, he also foresees that at the end of that purge there will still be glory on display in a new creation. Even though it will finally take the mighty power of God to renew the face of this earth, we even now try to live delightful lives of preservation for the same reasons that we try to live delightful lives of moral integrity. We do both as a participation in and an anticipation of the fullness of the kingdom *shalom* still to come. We live thus as a way to get ready for the kingdom.

Peter clamps together the two big themes of the Bible: creation and redemption, twin themes properly yoked. Our hope of redemption in Jesus, the Word made flesh, is anchored to and bolstered by our joy in the creation. For we were created to take joy in God's creation. Thus, it is only appropriate that even our hopes for paradise be more earthly and less heavenly. We often say that we "go to heaven" when we die. True enough, but Peter would remind us that the "heaven" God is preparing for us is a "new heaven *and a new earth*" — a new creation that will bear striking resemblance to this creation, but with a difference: It will be landscaped with righteousness, laid out according to the designs of *shalom.*

As Anthony Hoekema once noted, even the apostle John's apocalyptic vision in Revelation 21 tells us that when Christ returns, the new holy city of God's kingdom will come down out of heaven and descend to the earth. God's kingdom will be *here* and will include the trees, rivers, mountains, and oceans we see around us today. But it will be a renewed world in which all will be webbed together in mutually edifying relationships of wholeness and delight. A world like this one but deeper and richer in every sense.

C. S. Lewis painted a picture of this for us in the conclusion of the Chronicles of Narnia. Aslan the Lion takes the children into a new world. Following a great conflagration of fire and wind, the children and animals blink open their eyes only to behold a New Narnia — a world strangely familiar and yet one in which every blade of grass and every leaf on every tree seems to mean more. Everything is deeper. In fact, they discover that the farther they penetrate into the New Narnia, the deeper it becomes. The deeper they go, the more the world opens itself up to them.

And then with great delight they stamp their feet and dance with joy, recognizing that this, *this* is the world they had been made for. This is the world that had been their true home all along, the one they had been seeking even when they did not half-know what they were seeking. This world, landscaped with righteousness, is home. For here they feel they are inside joy; this is a place where joy is like a blanket to wrap yourself up in. Everything means more, for there is more to everything. [3]

So it will be in the new creation of our God. In Lewis's imaginative description of the New Narnia, he shows us the children tasting the glorious fruit of the New Narnia's trees. But Lewis does not try to describe how it tastes, for there is no way to describe so wondrous a thing. But, he says, suffice it to say that compared with this new fruit, the juiciest orange you ever had is dry, the most melting pear is hard and woody, the sweetest strawberry is sour. And if you want to know more than that, he says, you will just have to travel to this new country and taste for yourself.

One day we will. We can hardly wait. Far from dwindling, our appetite for God's creation goodness should be whetted more and more each day as we explore the richness of his world. As Peter wrote near the end of his own life, we look forward to the day of the Lord and to that land where righteousness and joy, delight and holiness, will be right at home — and so will we.

Epilogue

The Way It's Supposed to Be

For his book on sin, *Not the Way It's Supposed to Be,* Neal Plantinga took both his title and his opening illustration from the fine film *Grand Canyon.* [1] In the film's opening scene we see a well-to-do lawyer named Mack experience the ultimate urban nightmare. One dark night his car inexplicably sputters to a halt smack in the middle of a south-central Los Angeles neighborhood. Mack is soon accosted by some young street toughs who call him names, shove him around, and ominously hint at yet greater harm to follow.

But suddenly Mack is rescued by a tow-truck driver named Simon, who negotiates with the chief thug to let them go their way unharmed. At one point the thug asks Simon why this request should be granted, to which Simon replies, "Man, everything is supposed to be different than it is. Maybe you don't know that, but this is not the way it's supposed to be. I'm supposed to be able to do my job without *asking* you if I can. And this guy is supposed to be able to wait with his car without you ripping him off. Everything's supposed to be different than it is." As Plantinga put it, that assessment of life makes this tow-truck driver an heir of Saint Augustine. Indeed, because of sin very little in this world is exactly the way it is supposed to be according to God's design and intention.

Following this opening scene, the balance of *Grand Canyon* pummels viewers with still more images of life's disjointedness. Through a mind-numbing battery of vignettes and images, filmmaker Lawrence Kasdan paints a grim picture of urban loneliness, unrest, and squalor. We meet Simon's nephew, a good-looking yet hardened teenager who spends his nights "gang-banging." At one point Simon begs him to start doing something different with his life.

"Do you still want to be gang-banging when you're twenty-five?"

The youth replies with sad resignation, "Man, I'll never live to be twenty-five." Later that night the boy's mother and little sister are nearly killed when a rival gang sprays their house with automatic weapons fire.

The film also gives glimpses — often brief ones — of babies abandoned underneath shrubs, of wild-eyed, filthy hobos who live in cardboard boxes. We are also shown some striking contrasts: On the one hand we see impoverished inner-city teens who shoot each other over a pair of shoes; on the other we meet a wealthy entertainment mogul who gets rich by making movies that exploit and glorify such violence. On the one hand we see some lonely people desperate for a little human companionship, but on the other hand we meet well-off, happily married people who nevertheless wonder if the fleetingness of this life is all that there is.

Two motifs pervade the movie. One is visual: a police helicopter reappearing overhead both day and night as a deafening, whirling reminder of the violence and potential violence among which we live. The other is a question each of the characters asks again and again: "What's going on in this world?" In the wake of so much violence, despair, and squalor, the film's characters cannot help but ponder where society is headed. To them the whole world appears to be going down the toilet.

Few recent films have underscored so well the depraved nature of this world. But I mention it because of how the movie ends. Through a series of events, the film's main characters get to know each other — the inner-city gangbanger, the well-to-do lawyer and his wife, the tow-truck driver. After getting acquainted, they take a trip together to see the Grand Canyon in Arizona.

Suddenly and inexplicably, as they stand on the rim of this awesome spectacle of the creation, much of the crookedness within them straightens out. Suddenly these confused people gain a moment of clarity as the chaos of their lives is strangely hushed by the splendid cosmos of creation. Even the hard lines on the gangbanger's face soften in wonder, making him look young and full of promise, the way a teenager should look.

In a film bristling with well-written, snappy dialogue, this final scene is nearly silent. As the camera pans across their serene, smiling faces, the only sounds are a gentle wisp of wind and the songs of the birds. The only words spoken are simple yet profound. Simon asks Mack, "Well, what do you think?" Mack replies, "I think … it's not all bad."

For the first time in the film rays of hope flood the screen. But what is so very splendid for us Christians to note is that this hope grows out of the creation of our God. For when placed next to the film's opening scene, the message of this closing scene seems to be that if the rough-and-tumble violence of south-central

L.A. is not the way it's supposed to be, then something about creation's grandeur *is* the way it's supposed to be.

Much of what has been rattled apart within our souls by this brutal world somehow gets quietly reassembled in the face of God's handiwork. In the face of the creation and the power it conveys, we see indeed that "it's not all bad" — not now, not ever. It's not all bad because a Creator God, not a police helicopter, is what soars over our heads, assuring us that we are not alone. God will not abandon the work of his hands.

If Simon's assessment of the world in the opening scene makes him an heir of Saint Augustine, then Mack's comment in the closing scene makes him an heir of the apostles Paul and Peter. Their New Testament writings make clear that fallen, harsh, and brutal though this world is, the hope of a new creation has been sown into the soil of this world. The heartbeat of hope throbs at the center of every distant quasar and can be heard in every beating of the hummingbird's wings. "The creation will be liberated from its bondage to decay," Paul promises. "In keeping with [God's] promise we are looking forward to a new heaven and a new earth, the home of righteousness," Peter says.

Hints and whispers of this glory can be seen now, if only we take the time to notice. And when we do notice, we, like the people in *Grand Canyon,* will find that the rough places will become plain, the crooked will be made straight, the wilderness will bloom, the wrinkles of our souls will be ironed out even as the squalor of our minds is quieted by the creation's grandeur and by the holiness of him who is the Creator.

Notes

Introduction

1. *Christianity Today* 41, no. 5 (28 April 1997): pp. 12–13.
2. Eugene Peterson, *The Contemplative Pastor: Returning to the Art of Spiritual Direction* (Carol Stream, Ill.: Christianity Today, 1989), p. 78.

Chapter 1: Delightful Theology

1. Elizabeth Achtemeier, *Nature, God, and Pulpit* (Grand Rapids: Eerdmans, 1992), p. 27.
2. James L. Guth and Lyman A. Kellstedt, "How Green Is My Pulpit?" *Books and Culture* 2, no. 3 (May-June 1996), pp. 12–13.
3. Robert Booth Fowler, *The Greening of Protestant Thought* (Chapel Hill: University of North Carolina Press, 1995), pp. 13–19.
4. Booth Fowler, *Greening,* pp. 45–57.
5. Quoted in Steven Bouma-Prediger, *The Greening of Theology: The Ecological Models of Rosemary Radford-Ruether, Joseph Sittler, and Jürgen Moltmann* (Atlanta: Scholars Press, 1995), p. 265.
6. Quoted in Bernhard Anderson, *From Creation to New Creation* (Minneapolis: Fortress Press, 1994), p. 82.
7. Material drawn from Leo Perdue, *Wisdom and Creation: The Theology of Wisdom Literature* (Nashville: Abingdon Press, 1994), pp. 22–26.
8. Ibid., p. 34.
9. Robert Whelan, Joseph Kirwan, and Paul Haffner, *The Cross and the Rainforest: A Critique of Radical Green Spirituality* (Grand Rapids: The Acton Institute/Eerdmans, 1996), p. xi.
10. Cornelius Plantinga Jr., "Intellectual Love" (opening convocation sermon delivered at Calvin College, Grand Rapids, Mich., September 9, 1996).
11. James Nash, *Loving Nature: Ecological Integrity and Christian Responsibility* (Nashville: Abingdon Press, 1991), pp. 140–41.
12. Bill McKibben, *The Comforting Whirlwind: God, Job, and the Scale of Creation* (Grand Rapids: Eerdmans, 1994), p. 18.

13. For the material on the Book of Genesis, I am indebted to a couple of commentaries that, over the years, have informed my thinking and preaching: Walter Brueggemann, *Genesis* (Atlanta: John Knox Press, 1982), and Gordon Wenham, *Genesis 1–15* (Waco: Word Books, 1987). Many of Bruggemann's and Wenham's insights are scattered and interwoven in these pages.

14. Brueggemann, *Genesis*, pp. 36–37.

15. Ibid., p. 37.

16. Daniel Migliore, *Faith Seeking Understanding: An Introduction to Christian Theology* (Grand Rapids: Eerdmans, 1991), p. 93.

17. Terrence Fretheim, "The Reclamation of Creation," *Interpretation* 45, no. 4 (October 1991), p. 359. See also Terrence Fretheim, *Exodus* (Louisville: John Knox Press, 1991).

18. Larry Rasmussen, "Earth Faith" (lecture delivered at St. Olaf College, July 22, 1997). My thanks to Neal Plantinga for providing me with the information in Dr. Rasmussen's speech.

19. See Patrick Henry, "Singing the Faith Together," *The Christian Century* 114, no. 17 (21–28 May 1997), p. 500.

Chapter 2: Let's Play

1. Quoted in Sallie McFague, *The Body of God: An Ecological Theology* (Minneapolis: Augsburg Press, 1993), p. 51.

2. Elizabeth Achtemeier, *Nature, God, and Pulpit* (Grand Rapids: Eerdmans, 1992), p. 2.

3. Edwin McDowell, "Nature Is Second Fiddle to Dolly's Theme Park," *New York Times,* 14 August 1997, p. C4.

4. Fred Van Dyke, David Mahan, Joseph K. Sheldon, Raymond H. Brand, *Redeeming Creation: The Biblical Basis for Environmental Stewardship* (Downers Grove, Ill.: InterVarsity Press, 1996), p. 167.

5. John Calvin, *The Institutes of the Christian Religion* (Philadelphia: Westminster Press, 1960), I.XIV.21, pp. 180–81.

6. James Nash, *Loving Nature: Ecological Integrity and Christian Responsibility* (Nashville: Abingdon Press, 1991), p. 157.

7. Quoted in McFague, *Body of God*, pp. 209–10.

8. Thomas V. Morris, *Making Sense of It All: Pascal and the Meaning of Life* (Grand Rapids: Eerdmans, 1992), p. 44.

9. Maya Angelou, *Wouldn't Take Nothing for My Journey Now* (New York: Random House, 1993), p. 73.

10. Sallie McFague, *Super, Natural Christians: How We Should Love Nature* (Minneapolis: Fortress Press, 1997), pp. 170–71.

11. Bernhard Anderson, *From Creation to New Creation* (Minneapolis: Fortress Press, 1994), p. 155.

12. Francis Schaeffer, "Pollution and the Death of Man," in *A Christian View of the West*, vol. 5 of *The Complete Works of Francis Schaeffer: A Christian Worldview* (Westchester, Ill.: Crossway Books, 1982), pp. 32, 43.

13. Calvin B. DeWitt, *Earth-Wise: A Biblical Response to Environmental Issues* (Grand Rapids: CRC Publications, 1994), pp. 59–72.

14. C. S. Lewis, *The Screwtape Letters* (New York: Collier/Macmillan Publishers, 1982), pp. 15–17.

15. Calvin, *Institutes*, I.V.4, pp. 55–56.

16. Information drawn from Martin E. Marty's newsletter *Context*, 1 December 1990.

Chapter 3: Hearing Creation's Chorus

1. C. S. Lewis, *That Hideous Strength* (New York: Collier/Macmillan Publishers, 1946), p. 172.

2. Calvin B. DeWitt, "Praising Rembrandt but Despising His Paintings: Stewardship of God's Creation" (speech delivered at Calvin College, Grand Rapids, Mich., January 7, 1997).

3. My source for the information on Gaia comes from Stephen Bede Scharper, *Redeeming the Time: A Political Theology of the Environment* (New York: Continuum Books, 1997), pp. 54–55.

4. Cf. Sallie McFague, *The Body of God: An Ecological Theology* (Minneapolis: Augsburg Press, 1993).

5. Frederick Buechner, "Message in the Stars," in *The Magnificent Defeat* (San Francisco: Harper and Row, 1966), pp. 44–50.

6. C. S. Lewis, *Meditations on the Psalms* (New York: Harcourt, Brace, and World, 1958), pp. 82–89.

7. Jürgen Moltmann, *The Way of Jesus Christ: Christology in Messianic Directions* (San Francisco: Harper Collins, 1990), pp. 307–12.

8. Robert Whelan, Joseph Kirwan, and Paul Haffner, *The Cross and the Rainforest: A Critique of Radical Green Spirituality* (Grand Rapids: The Acton Institute/Eerdmans, 1996), p.112.

9. Ibid., p. 111.

10. Ibid., p. 118.

11. Ibid., pp. 7–8.

12. David Mc Collough, *Truman* (New York: Simon and Schuster, 1992), p. 104.

Chapter 4: Bearing God's Image in the Creation

1. Charles Krauthammer, "Saving Nature, but Only for Man," *Time*, 17 June 1991, p. 82.

2. Robert Whelan, Joseph Kirwan, and Paul Haffner, *The Cross and the Rainforest: A Critique of Radical Green Spirituality* (Grand Rapids: The Acton Institute/Eerdmans, 1996), p. x.

3. Ibid., pp. 64–66.

4. Sallie McFague, *The Body of God: An Ecological Theology* (Minneapolis: Augsburg Press, 1993), p. 112.

5. Ibid., p. 6.

6. Cf. Stephen Bede Scharper, *Redeeming the Time: A Political Theology of the Environment* (New York: Continuum Books, 1997).

7. Calvin B. DeWitt, *Earth-Wise: A Biblical Response to Environmental Issues* (Grand Rapids: CRC Publications, 1994), pp. 40–41.

8. Lynn White Jr., "The Historic Roots of Our Ecologic Crisis," in Francis Schaeffer, "Pollution and the Death of Man" in *A Christian View of the West*, vol. 5 of *The Complete Works of Francis Schaeffer: A Christian Worldview* (Westchester, Ill.: Crossway Books, 1982), pp. 57–69.

9. E. Calvin Beisner, *Where Garden Meets Wilderness: Evangelical Entry into the Environmental Debate* (Grand Rapids: Action Institute/Eerdmans, 1997), p. 13.

10. Sallie McFague, *Super, Natural Christians: How We Should Love Nature* (Minneapolis: Fortress Press, 1997), p. 64.

11. Richard Mouw, *Distorted Truth: What Every Christian Needs to Know about the Battle for the Mind* (San Francisco: Harper and Row, 1989), p. 81.

12. Ibid., pp. 81–82.

Chapter 5: Preserving Creation's Chorus

1. Frederick Buechner, *The Longing for Home* (San Francisco: Harper Collins, 1996), p. 127.

2. Ibid., 127.

3. Robert Whelan, Joseph Kirwan, and Paul Haffner, *The Cross and the Rainforest: A Critique of Radical Green Spirituality* (Grand Rapids: The Acton Institute/Eerdmans, 1996), p. 69.

4. Steven Bouma-Prediger, *The Greening of Theology: The Ecological Models of Rosemary Radford-Ruether, Joseph Sittler, and Jürgen Moltmann* (Atlanta: Scholars Press, 1995), p. 281.

5. C. S. Lewis, *Letters to Malcom, Chiefly on Prayer: Reflections on the Dialogue between God and Man* (New York: Harcourt, Brace, Jovanovich, 1964), p. 74.

6. Whelan, Kirwan, and Haffner, *Cross and the Rainforest,* p. 40

7. Anthony Hoekema, *The Bible and the Future* (Grand Rapids: Eerdmans, 1979), p. 281.

8. Francis Schaeffer, "Pollution and the Death of Man," in *A Christian View of the West,* vol. 5 of *The Complete Works of Francis Schaeffer: A Christian Worldview* (Westchester, Ill.: Crossway Books, 1982), pp. 4, 19.

9. Matt Ridely and Bobbi S. Low, "Can Selfishness Save the Environment?" *The Atlantic Monthly,* September 1993.

10. Quoted in Fred Van Dyke, David Mahan, Joseph K. Sheldon, Raymond H. Brand, *Redeeming Creation: The Biblical Basis for Environmental Stewardship* (Downers Grove, Ill.: InterVarsity Press, 1996), p. 138.

11. Calvin B. DeWitt, *Earth-Wise: A Biblical Response to Environmental Issues* (Grand Rapids: CRC Publications, 1994), p. 52.

12. Sallie McFague, *Super, Natural Christians: How We Should Love Nature* (Minneapolis: Fortress Press, 1997), p. 40.

13. Bruce Babbit, "Stewards of Creation," *Christian Century* 113, no. 16 (8 May 1996), p. 500.

Chapter 6: The Landscape of Righteousness

1. John Updike, *Toward the End of Time* (New York: Alfred Knopf, 1997), p. 3.

2. Eugene Peterson, *The Message: The New Testament in Contemporary English* (Colorado Springs: NavPress Publishing Group, 1993), pp. 498–99.

3. C. S. Lewis, *The Last Battle* (New York: Collier/Macmillan Publishers, 1956), pp. 161ff.

Epilogue

1. Cornelius Plantinga Jr., *Not the Way It's Supposed to Be: A Breviary of Sin* (Grand Rapids: Eerdmans, 1995).

Subject Index

SCRIPTURE INDEX

COLOPHON

Type was set in 11-point Garamond on 13-point leading.
This book was produced by Aaron Phipps
with a Power Macintosh 7100/66 computer using
Quark XPress 3.31.

✝